D1108594

HUMAN RELATIONS AND THE SOUTH AFRICAN SCENE IN THE LIGHT OF SCRIPTURE

Official translation of the report
**Ras, Volk en Nasie
en Volkereverhoudinge
in die lig van die Skrif**
approved and accepted
by the General Synod
of the Dutch Reformed Church
October 1974

Dutch Reformed Church Publishers
Cape Town - Pretoria

Published on behalf of
the General Synod of the
Dutch Reformed Church
Set in 10 on 11 pt Times Roman Monotype
Printed and bound by
National Book Printers Ltd.
Elsies River, Cape, 1976

ISBN 0 86991 158 9

Contents

Introduction

About 42 % of the White population of the Republic of South Africa are members of the Dutch Reformed Church (Nederduitse Gereformeerde Kerk). As a result of its missionary endeavours, 14 younger Churches were established amongst the Black, Brown and Asian population groups within and beyond the borders of the Republic. At present these Churches have a total of 1 640 367 adherents – already about 400 000 more than the number of Whites belonging to the Dutch Reformed Church.

The Dutch Reformed Church is a direct continuation of the Reformed religion of the first White colonists who came to South Africa in 1652. As the Church representing the greater majority of Dutch-speaking (and later Afrikaans-speaking) citizens of South Africa, its very existence is inseverable from the whole of our country's chequered history. In times of danger the Church was both consolation and anchor to the lonely frontier farmers. The Voortrekkers took the Bible with them into the hostile interior, and on the way even organised a "travelling congregation". Since the beginning of South African history this Church has had to grapple with the problems of a multinational and multiracial country. Over the years practical methods have been found to preach the Gospel to people of widely divergent languages, cultures and levels of civilization "so that each man could hear and preach, in his own language, the great deeds of God" (Mission Order, section 1.4.) As a result of a natural process of growth, separate churches were established amongst the various population groups. The progress of these churches was so blessed, and the results so positive, that this method has had a considerable influence on later political thinking and developments.

It follows that the church has always been intimately involved in the constitutional development of our country. The Church has been giving constant attention to the demands of the Word of God in the particular situation of South Africa. Successive Church congresses and synodal meetings have discussed the issues involved in depth. Since the 1930's the Church has continually expressed itself on the Christian implications of "apartheid", "separate development", "autogenous development" or whatever form the political thinking of the people of the country has assumed from time to time.

The report presented here is the result of careful consideration and reflection. It represents convictions existing in the Dutch Reformed Church with regard to the problem of relationships in a multinational country, as seen from the point of view of the eternal and immutable norms of the Word of God.

It is the result of collaboration between professors of theology, teaching staff at our theological institutions and leading figures in the ministry and mission fields.

It was submitted to the General Synod of the Dutch Reformed Church during its session in Cape Town from 16 to 25 October, 1974. The Synod dealt with certain propositions (portions of the report printed in bold type) and arrived at certain conclusions concerning those propositions.

It merely took note of the portions printed in medium type, i.e. the explanations and motivations of the propositions, and referred these to the Executive Council for final formulation.

The report is presented here in its final processed form in the hope that it may contribute to a better understanding of the Dutch Reformed Church and serve as a profitable basis for discussion in the Church as well as for discussion with other Churches and Christians within and beyond the borders of our country.

The Executive Council:

D. P. M. Beukes	Chairman
J. D. Vorster	Vice-chairman
J. E. Potgieter	Secretary
F. E. O'B. Geldenhuys	Actuary
S. J. Eloff	
P. C. van Rooyen	
J. T. Jordaan	
D. du P. Moolman	
A. van der Merwe	
A. F. Louw	
H. D. A. du Toit	
D. S. Snyman	

Pretoria
March 1975

Chapter 1

General Remarks

1. Need for Constant Reflection

The Church can never allow itself the luxury of regarding its consideration of relations between races and peoples as completed. A finding in
the REPORT OF THE AD HOC COMMISSION OF THE
COUNCIL OF CHURCHES, 1956, is pertinent in this regard: "To
an increasing extent the Christian Church is becoming aware of the
danger of acquiescing in race relations which possibly do not accord
with the Word of God. That is why the Dutch Reformed Church is
listening anew to what the Word of God has to tell us about the matter
in the present-day situation" (Doctrinal Approach, proposition 6).
This finding will always be of current interest to the Church, firstly
because it will always be the calling of the Church to listen anew to
the Word of God; and secondly, because the "present situation" is not
static, but part of the dynamic process of change which is characteristic
of our age; and, thirdly, because the Church must constantly ask
itself whether previous findings on relations between races and peoples
are, in fact, in all respects "in accordance with the Word of God".

2. Word of God as Premise and Norm

In its consideration of relations between races and peoples, the Church
of Jesus Christ must accept the Word of God as premise and norm.
The object of this study is to focus the light of the Scriptures on relations between races and peoples. Hereby we profess the conviction
that the Holy Scriptures contains the principles normative for all
spheres of life, therefore also for relations between peoples and
races, and that the Church of Jesus Christ must unconditionally and
obediently bow to these principles.
In this connection the Church of Jesus Christ must maintain un-
flinching honesty and be prepared to look critically at itself. There is
a very real danger that the Church, imagining itself obedient to the
Scriptures, may in reality bow to some other authority, for example
some humanistic-liberalistic ideal; the voice of a specific people or
political party; the pressures of economic or emotional factors, etc.
Only when our convictions and actions are founded on the rock of
the World will they be able to weather the storms (Matt. 7 : 24 et
seq.).

7

3. Definition of Concepts

A fruitful discussion of the problem in question is only possible when we have a clear understanding of the terms race, people and nation. Despite a certain difference of opinion, most scientists distinguish the concepts as follows: "race" is a biological, "people" a cultural and "nation" a political concept. These concepts can be more closely defined as follows: **Race** (the etimology of the word is uncertain – Boshoff-Nienaber: **Afrikaanse Etimologieë** (1967), p. 532) signifies a group of people classified into one catagory on the basis of identical hereditary characteristics, for example colour of hair, skin and eyes, shape of mouth, face and hair, structure of the cranium, physique. Such characteristics must be inborn and hereditary. It is important to note that for a person to belong to a specific race, these characteristics must appear, not in isolation, but in a specific combination.

A single characteristic, for example skin colour, is not sufficient to indicate that the person with that characteristic belongs to a particular race. This characteristic must consistently appear with other specific characteristics, for example colour of eyes, hair type, structure of the cranium and physique. In addition, it must be pointed out that we are not dealing here with complete similarities; we are only dealing with averages. Characteristics differ within the same race, and therefore average resemblances are used to determine a particular racial type. We may therefore state the position as follows: "It is the sum total of the characteristics appearing **together** in a particular **combination of averages,** and not seperate, absolute characteristics, which determines the race group to which a person belongs".

A people is a group of individuals who are classified as belonging to a particular group on the basis of a common culture, i.e. a group of individuals who share a common language, habits, general lifestyle, etc.

The difference between the characteristics of races and peoples is chiefly that in the former case the characteristics are hereditary and cannot be adopted or discarded at will by the individual, while in the latter case the characteristics can be relinquished at will and the individual can therefore exchange one national community for another.

The concensus of scientific opinion is that the term **nation** has political significance, indicating a group subject to the same central authority. These definitions and distinctions are of importance in gaining a better insight into the nature of the problem we are dealing with in this report.

8

4. Nature of the Problem

A balanced and careful analysis of the nature of the problem of relations in the context of the world situation is of vital importance for a correct insight into the manner in which the problem should be solved. The fact that the problem of relations originates in racial contrasts cannot be denied, but at the same time the significance of racial contrasts as supposed cause of the majority of the world's problems in regard to relationships is completely exaggerated. The exaggerated emphasis on the racial aspect of world tensions not only blocks efforts to solve the world's problems, but is also essentially one-sided and naive.

The problems of relations throughout the world today are far too complex to be based solely on racial contrasts. J. H. Coetzee points out that the world's great population problems can be reduced, in the first instance, to conflict and hostility between peoples and, in the second instance, to the problem of "over-population" with its concomitant poverty and hunger. (Bevolkingsvraagstukke: Oorsig en Perspektief: **Die Atoomeeu in U Lig,** 1969.) Not all conflicts and tensions between peoples are based on racial contrasts. He further points out that the two-fold problem of over-population and hunger at present is eagerly ascribed to simple factors such as colonialist and capitalist exploitation. He rightly states that for the most part the problem cannot be solved that easily. "Actually, these phenomena only become vital factors under specific circumstances . . . The basic cause should rather be sought in the cultural lag of the relevant people and in the petrification of its cultural structure and customs." The solution of the world's problems is not promoted by elevating a single factor to the level of an all-prevailing cause and remedy. In order to apply the correct therapy in the light of the Scriptures, the "malady" of the world's relations between races and peoples must be comprehensively and correctly diagnosed.

5. Hermeneutic approach

We can only truly discern what the Scriptures teach on relations between races and peoples if we correctly interpret and utilise the Scriptures. The Bible was never intended to be used as a scientific text-book for sociology and anthropology. Also, one must avoid the danger of allowing the "historic situation" to function as a hermeneutic principle according to which the Scriptures are interpreted. Although the Bible is not a scientific text-book, it nevertheless presents fundamental data and principles which are of normative significance in all spheres of life. However, in our derivation and formulation of such "principles" we must guard against "an incautious use of the term 'principle'" (G.E.S., Grand Rapids, 1963). In its handling of Scriptural data the Church will constantly have to be aware of the central theme of its preaching, i.e. proclaiming the way of salvation in Christ and the coming of the Kingdom of God to His glory. This means that the Church will indicate and proclaim the norms applicable in all spheres of life, commend that which accords with this theme in given circumstances and give warning when the way of salvation is blocked in some or other way and the ethical norms of the Scriptures for all spheres of life are not being honoured.

A serious warning must be issued against the marked tendency which has always existed, namely to link-up an understanding of the Bible with current tradition. The danger then exists of the Scriptures being interpreted according to what the "historical situation" prescribes – and therefore mostly on a selective basis. In his book **The Authority of the Old Testament,** John Bright calls attention to this dangerous misuse of the Scriptures, and illustrates it with reference to efforts by an earlier generation to justify slavery on Scriptural grounds (pp. 46-51).

An obvious but important consideration is that our use of the Scriptures must not be biblicistic. At all times individual texts must be interpreted in their context and in conjunction with the whole of revelation history, i.e. the history of the unfolding of God's redemptive purpose for his chosen people. Among other things, this means that the unity of the Scriptures must be taken into account, including the special nature of the relationship between Old Testament and New Testament. The relationship between the Old Testament and New Testament is marked not only by the continuity of revelation history, but also by its discontinuity, and both aspects should be given well-grounded consideration.

Although the Bible is no scientific text-book, it nevertheless does present fundamental data and principles which are of normative significance in all spheres of life. This is linked up with the fact that the central theme of Scriptures is the Kingdom of God and that Christ's incarnation and sacrifice of atonement also have wider cosmic significance. In assessing the directive principles for all spheres of life as derived from Scriptural data, we must take into account the timely warning of the Reformed Ecumenical Synod of Grand Rapids, 1963, against "an incautious use of the term 'principle'". They explain: "When the Synod uses the term 'principle' in this context the term shall mean a regulative rule of conduct expressive of God's will as revealed in Scripture, and demanding application regardless of place, time and circumstance" (Acts, p.37).

Finally, we do bear in mind that Scriptural data is used by het Church to determine its standpoint and attitude in respect of the problem of relations between races and peoples. In this respect we do not expect the Church to differ essentially from politicians, lawyers or sociologists who believe in the Scriptures, but its language and emphasis will nevertheless differ, i.e. in accordance with the nature and limit of its prophetic preaching.

In its handling of Scriptural data the Church will constantly have to be aware of the central theme of its preaching, i.e. preaching the way of salvation in Christ and the coming of the kingdom of God. This means that the Church will have to indicate and proclaim the norms that accord with this theme in all spheres of life and give warning when the way to salvation is blocked in some way or other. In this respect the Church has, in its prophetic calling, a critical function in respect of the State and society, and it is part of its calling to cast the purifying light of the Word of God on all situations.

We proceed from the following hermeneutic principles:

The Bible must be interpreted in accordance with recognised, reformed, scientific, hermeneutic principles in keeping with its actual intention – it is not a scientific text-book for empirical sociology or anthropology. The Scriptures must not be used biblicistically – texts must be interpreted in their own context and in the context of the entire history of salvation.

Although the Bible is not a scientific text-book, it does nevertheless present fundamental data and principles of normative significance in all spheres of life, and this applies to relations between races and peoples as well.

In dealing with Scriptural data the Church will constantly have to be aware of the central theme of its preaching – i.e. the way of salvation in Christ and the coming of the kingdom of God – and it will have to indicate and extol the norms that coincide with this theme in all spheres of life.

On the other hand the Church has a prophetic function in respect of the state and society when the Scriptural norms that should apply in all spheres of life are not respected.

In the implementation of this function the Church must guard against two extremes: on the one hand it must guard against a lack of daring, and on the other hand against a lack of discretion. The Church must not adapt itself to such an extent as to forfeit confidence, but neither may it act without pastoral compassion and understanding.

11

6. Limitation of material and method of treatment

The positive right of limiting Scriptural data to those principles which have normative significance within the total context of Biblical preaching, and the method of systematising data on particular themes, cannot be denied.

The revelation of God in the Scriptures has come to us in the language of men and couched in history. This means that in His acts of revelation God has linked up with the fulness and richness of human life, also as it found expression in the family, group and nation. The Bible presents a variety of historical and archaeological data as well as data which reveal God's purpose of salvation for His chosen people, all of which in some way or another illuminate how the peoples of those times lived. Thanks to the results of excavations, it is at present possible to gain a clearer insight into the socio-historical pattern of existence of the peoples of those times. It is self-evident that we do not have to go into all of that data. Much of the data in the Scriptures and in sources outside the Bible is merely descriptive, and although it is of interest in determining the contours of social patterns in those times, we would rather concentrate on viewpoints that have normative significance for us in Biblical preaching as a whole.

7. Use of the terms 'am, gôi, etc.

The Bible does, it is true, use a number of terms such as 'am, gôi, etc., to indicate certain groupings of individuals, but this usage is not consistent throughout and often serves to denote the significance the words have gained within the unique purpose and meaning of the Bible as God's revelation of His redemptive plan. Nowhere does the Bible use the word "race" or any word to express this concept in terms of our scientific definition.

In respect of the concept "race" therefore, our investigation of Scriptural data leads us to a chiefly negative result. Anthropologically the characteristic racial differences never played a decisive role. This means that principles, as the term had been defined by the Reformed Ecumenical Synod of Grand Rapids, should here be applied with caution. In terms of race relations the Scriptures never present "a regulative rule of conduct expressive of Gods wil . . . and demanding application regardless of place, time, and circumstance."

In the Old Testament the situation is somewhat different with respect to the terms "people" and "nation". According to Speiser

12

the word 'am is chiefly used to designate a genetically related group while gôi chiefly typifies a political entity centered in a particular residential area. He rightly comments: "These terms may be interchanged, yet the underlying distinction is still apparent for the most part" ("Ethnic Divisions of Man", in **The Interpreter's Dictionary of the Bible,** Part III, p. 236. Abingdon Press, USA, 1962.)

It is clear, however, that the use of these two terms in the Old Testament is not based on a scientific definition; their meaning is derived from salvation history.

Our conclusion is that the terms, as used in the Bible, cannot simply be transferred to our present situation as far as races and peoples are concerned, firstly, because the Scriptures evidence no racial problems and, secondly, because the terms "people" and "nation" have a primarily historico-redemptive meaning.

8. Unity of mankind

The Scriptures teach and uphold the essential unity of mankind and the primordial relatedness and fundamental equality of all peoples. The "genealogical table of peoples" of Gen. 10 uniquely emphasises the unity of mankind. It was not the intention to present the genealogical register of a certain nation; the intention was to indicate how all the nations are descended from Noah. Hugo du Plessis **(Banier van die Volke, p. 38)** states the case in the following words: "What is given here is the genealogy of the human race in its differentiation into nations . . . in spite of the God-willed diversity, there is not only the unity of common descent from Noah, but here we also find, at least in principle, complete equality of the generations. All the peoples bear the same relationship to God and are answerable to God in the same way. Here all ethnocentrism is transcended." He then goes on to state: "This majestic vision of the primordial relatedness of all peoples and their fundamental equality is only found in the Scriptures" (op. cit. p. 38 et seq.).

The "genealogical table of peoples" is therefore of importance, not only from the point of view of ethnic diversity, but also to the basic unity of all generations and humanity as a whole.

Differentiation comes about because of distinctions in races and peoples, but differentiation does not revoke the essential unity. Nor can races and peoples be compared with one another and classified in order of superiority, inferiority or difference in kind. Such distinctions smack of heathenism because they do not respect the Biblical foudation of man's descent from one human couple.

9. Ethnic diversity

The Scriptures also teach and uphold the ethnic diversity of the human race.

Ethnic diversity does not have a polyphylogenetic origin. Whether or not the differentiation process first started with Babel, or whether it was already implicit in the fact of Creation and the cultural injunction (Genesis 1 : 28), makes no essential difference to the conclusion that ethnic diversity is in its very origin in accordance with the will of God for this dispensation. The choice between these alternative explanations of origins depends on an examination of the important chapters 10 and 11 of the book of Genesis. The universal message of the "genealogical table of peoples" (Gen. 10) is that God created all peoples from one progenitor, and that this view of the human race not only avoids the danger of ethnocentrism, but also that of cosmopolitanism. Gen. 10 and 11, which should be read in conjunction, each individually recounts the fact and process of the division and distribution of peoples. According to Gen. 10, the diversity of peoples is the result of a progressive split in the genealogical line, while Gen. 11 : 1-9 presents it as being the result of dispersal. The two processes are not unrelated. In Gen. 11 the spontaneous development of generations is given its momentum and specific character. In the process of progressive differentiation of the human race into peoples and races there is not only a curse, but also a blessing, not only a judgment on the sinful arrogance of the builders of Babel, but also an active mercy preserving mankind from destruction so "That they should seek the Lord" (Acts. 17 : 27) and so that God's purpose for the fulfilment of the earth should be achieved. The question we are faced with here is whether the Scriptures also give us a normative indication of the way in which the human race differentiated into a variety of races, peoples and nations. It is therefore a question of whether the diversity of peoples accords with the will of God and whether it was God's intention, from the outset, to differentiate the human race in this way. If this question is answered in the affirmative, we already have an indication that we should judge and evaluate the existence of various races and peoples as a positive premise. A further question will involve, of course, the relationship between diversity and unity among peoples, and, in particular, how both should be judged in the context of the kingdom of God. This is of particular importance because of the difference in emphasis between ourselves and Christians of other countries. This difference relates to the manner in which we value the diversity of peoples positively and incorparate it in our ideas on relations between races and peoples. It is therefore important to distinguish carefully.

14

In this connection we must again refer to the so-called "genealogical table" (Gen. 10).

This genealogical table was not designed to be a comprehensive catalogue of all the possible tribes and nations that existed since the Flood and will exist until the Second Coming of Christ. Therefore every effort "to place all known peoples according to the genealogy of Gen. 10 is doomed to failure from the start, for the simple reason that it conflicts with the intention of our chapter" (Gen. 1, KV p. 265). The meaning of the "genealogical table of peoples" was to clarify for those for whom it was primarily written, how the known population of the earth stood, at the time, in relation to the sons of Noah. "And for all subsequent time there lies, in this limited reference, the proclamation that, along similar lines, the whole population of the earth is descended from the sons of Noah" (op. cit. p. 266).

From this "genealogical table of peoples" it is possible to deduce the following: The mythological idea of peoples being descended from the gods is here rooted out. The universal message of the "genealogical table of peoples" is that God let all peoples descend from one progenitor; it is not the intention to give the genealogical tree of one particular nation, but to indicate how all the nations had their origin in Noah; thus the emphasis falls here on the primordial relatedness of all peoples and their fundamental equivalence.

The differentiation into "nations" and "families" here takes place along the line of descent in the course of history (tôledôt). We can agree in part with the following comment of the Study Commission of the Reformed Churches in the Netherlands (1971): "If these peoples had continued, obedient to Gods ways, this family relationship would have remained characteristic of mutual relationships." The problem, however, is that Gen. 10 presupposes the confusion of tongues as a fact (cf. Gen. 10 : 25); it is also apparent that in the "genealogical table of peoples" "language" (lasjôn) is undeniably a principle of division. In any case, the view that the original human race, before the confusion of tongues, was only differentiated on a family basis, is a hypothesis which has no foundation in Gen. 10 Therefore we must consult Gen. 11 : 1-9 for more light on the origins of ethnic diversity.

9.1 The confusion of tongues (Gen. 11 : 1-9)

The event itself: It is important to note that the situation presupposed in Gen. 11 : 1-9 goes back beyond Gen. 10 and in reality links up with the end of Gen. 9. The decendants of Noah's three sons remained in the vicinity of Ararat for a few generations (Gen.

15

10 : 25) before they decided to move in a (south-) easterly direction to (the later) Babylonia (11 : 12). In the first verse these people are described as "the whole earth" in the sense of "all the inhabitants of the earth". It is important to note this. At the time, therefore, there were no other people on earth! It is also said that at that time they all spoke the same language. This state of affairs existed after their arrival in Babylonia and the commencement of their building program. Verse 6 states: "Behold the people ('am) is one and they have all one language."

These people clearly valued the unity of language and community because, apart from the motive of making a name for themselves, their city and tower had to serve specifically to prevent their being "scattered abroad upon the face of the whole earth" (v. 4).

From the sequel to this history is it clear that the undertaking and the intentions of these people where in conflict with the will of God. Apart from the reckless arrogance that is evident in their desire to make a name for themselves, the deliberate concentration on one spot was in conflict with God's command to replenish the earth (Gen. 1 : 28; 9 : 1, 7). The negative criticism of the actions of the tower builders is particularly apparent in what follows. God's perception of their efforts and intention leads to a judgement which was to affect human beings in the very structure of their community life: their **one** language was split up into a diversity of language, with the result that a communication crisis developed and it was impossible for them to associate meaningfully with one another. The result gives evidence of God's intention as far as they were concerned: "So the Lord scattered them abroad from thence upon the face of all the earth" (verses 8, 9).

The significance of this event: As far as the origin of diversity among races and peoples is concerned, the significance of this event can be both underrated and overrated. It is underrated by those who think that the division of languages had no appreciable effect on the differences between races and peoples. It is true that Gen. 11 : 1-9 does not mention **races** or even **peoples** in the plural. Here it is chiefly a question of the confusion of tongues. We must nevertheless bear two factors in mind: firstly the significance of language to the psychic structure of man – and therefore we can rightly speak of a "spiritual" splitting up of the human race, at the time, into seperate community units with the concomitant development of individual cultures and religions; secondly, that Gen. 11 : 1-9 gives an answer to the question about how the diversity of peoples, of which mention is made in Gen. 10, occurred. That the differentiation of humanity into various language groups and "nations" was extended further to give rise to **race** differences is not, in fact, mentioned in the Scriptures in so many words, but is nevertheless confirmed by the facts of history. The ancient Egyptians were already familiar with a division of mankind into (five!) races.

The significance of the story is overrated in a certain sense by those who think there would have been no question of a diversity of races and peoples if there had been no confusion of tongues. At the time, it is true, mankind had not yet differentiated biologically, politically or culturally into seperate community units. Then again, we have to acknowledge that the confusion of tongues gave a specific character and momentum to the process of differentiation. In this connection we shall constantly have to bear in mind the following considerations: firstly the fact, to which we have already referred, that diversity was implicit in the fact of Creation (Acts 17 : 26) and the cultural injunction (Gen. 1 : 28; 9 : 1, 7); secondly the fact that the confusion of tongues occurred at a time when the process of differentiation into separate "families" or community units had already, according to Gen. 10 : 25, been in progress for quite some time; thirdly it must be borne in mind that the process of progressive differentiation was hampered by the fact that the people of that time resisted it, as is evident from the fact that up to that stage they had also lived together in one geographic region (Gen. 11 : 2). In a certain sense, up to that moment in time the "unity" had been artificial and clearly in conflict with the intention that mankind should be spread across the face of the earth: Fourthly, we may not forget that sin as a dividing factor was not restricted to events at Babel (cf. Gen. 6); it therefore does not go without saying that the family relationship would have remained characteristic of mutual relationships if the confusion of tongues had not taken place; finally, it specifically strikes us that the judgement of the confusion of tongues was not "arbitrary", but resolved itself in the course of generations: the dispersal at Babel took place within the family divisions of the sons of Noah (cf. Gen. 10 : 25).

Additionally, in our assessment of the confusion of tongues, we must also bear in mind the following two factors: on the one hand the judgment in it. S. du Toit puts it this way: "As a result of the fact that the one could not understand the language of the other (Gen. 11 : 7), what would have been a natural differentiation became a division which resulted in continual tension and conflict among peoples, something which, according to the Scriptures, will endure to the very last" (**Openbaringsgeskiedenis van die O.T.** p. 119). On the other hand the confusion of tongues was also an act of mercy and blessing in as much as it guaranteed the continued existence of the human race and in as much as God achieved His purpose with the creation of the human race.

To arrive at the whole truth in connection with the family of nations, Gen. 10 and 11 must be read in conjunction. The progressive differentiation of humanity into peoples and races involved not only a curse, but also a blessing, not only a judgment on the sinful arrogance of the tower builders of Babel, but also an act of mercy whereby mankind is not only protected from destruction, but God's purpose with the creation of man is achieved. Zimmerli rightly states: "He who speaks only of blessings and ignores the curse, speaks falsely. But no less falsely speaks he who calls the diversity of peoples according to language, country and nation sinful. It is indicative of the sober balance of the Scriptures that it is as far removed from selfish nationalism as from a colourless internationalism." (quoted by Du Toit, op. cit., p. 119).

For the purpose of our report the question arises as to whether Gen. 11 : 1-9 can serve as a Scriptural basis for a policy of autogenous development? Our answer is a qualified yes. The diversity of races and peoples to which the confusion of tongues contributed, is an aspect of reality which God obviously intended for this dispensation. To deny this fact is to side with the tower builders. Therefore a policy which in broad terms (as distinct from its concrete implementation) bears this reality in mind, is Biblically realistic in the good sense of the word. We must not forget that Gen. 11 also tells us of man's attempt to establish a (forced) unity of the human race. Herewith we are not saying that no positive value attaches to attempts at achieving unity as such. The history of peoples in Biblical times, and particularly that of peoples in modern times, relates the process wherein smaller groups have become linked into larger units, and no one wishes to claim that these efforts have only furnished negative results. The endeavour towards unity by the tower builders of Babel, however, was rooted, not in a God-given command, but in sinful human arrogance. This form of unity carries within it the germ of its own destruction and can never be a substitute for the unity that God alone can give. Therefore, also from this point of view, there is reason to bear in mind the diversity of races and peoples.

We repeat however, that ours is a qualified "yes". Gen. 11 : 1-9 answers the question as to how, in terms of Gen. 10, the diversity of languages and nations originated. We have pointed out (2.3), however, that Gen. 10 also emphasises the primordial relatedness of all nations: everyone's genealogical history is traced back to one progenitor, Noah (10 : 1). In no instance does the diversity revoke the essential unity of the human race. In all races and peoples we are dealing with **individuals** "related" to one another on the horizontal plane, and on the vertical plane to God to whom they are accountable.

It is also of importance to note that Gen. 11 : 1-9 does not terminate the genealogical history in Gen. 10, but merely interrupts it! This story is taken up again in Gen. 11 : 10-12 : 3; the genealogical history of Shem culminates in the call to Abraham, the spiritual father of a new "people", **one** in Christ. This "unity" does not, in fact, obliterate language, cultural and racial differences, but transcends them – and that is why the policy of seperate development retains its relational validity, even in this new situation. In respect of the spiritual unity of the faithful among all peoples and races, any policy of seperate development is, in a certain sense, relative.

Gen. 11 : 1-9 therefore does have an important message as far as our realisation of realities of life is concerned, but at the same time it is not the highest or last word in the Scriptures. The highest and last word, in respect of the diversity of peoples, is spoken by the core of events forming the Crucifixion and resurrection of Christ and Pentecost, and focuses our attention on the new song that the redeemed of all peoples will sing at the Second Coming of Christ (Rev. 5 : 9).

9.2 The Noah prophecy (Gen. 9 : 24-27)

There is no Scriptural basis for relating the subordinate position of some present day peoples to the curse on Canaan.

This prophecy requires special attention in a consideration of the origin of nations. The classification of peoples (and races?) in accordance with the sons of Noah (Gen. 10) has had a marked influence on Western thinking on this issue. The three sons were thought to be the progenitors of the three main races: White, Black and Yellow (cf. E.N.S.I.E., VI, p. 238-243). Thus the temptation was there to relate the status and fate of the various races to the several pronouncements of Noah, with the implication that the Negroid races, as descendants of Ham, were doomed to perpetual servitude by the curse of Noah.

It simply is not true that Ham and all his descendants were for ever cursed: in the first place, the curse was specifically limited to Canaan and therefore does not apply to the other sons of Ham. Moreover, all that was said was that Canaan would become a servant of Shem and Japheth (Gen. 9 : 25-27). Ham is therefore punished in his eldest son, and the punishment is applicable only to the Canaanites. This prophecy was later fulfilled in that the Canaanites became servants of the Israelites.

The curse on the son of Ham must not lead us to believe that all his descendants were for ever excluded from the benefits of our specific grace. The prophecy is indeed conditional. If the Hamites should be converted, they would also share in the blessing promised to Abraham and, through him, to all subsequent generations. 'For the Hamite peoples, too, there is room by Jesus' cross . . .' (Aalders, K.V., p. 262 et seq.).

In the light of the foregoing, there is therefore no Scriptural foundation on which the subordinate position of some present-day peoples, which is the result of all sorts of historical and cultural factors, can be related to the curse on Canaan and, consequently, be perpetuated through all future. We agree with S. du Toit when he says: 'We must also state that the well-known conception that the natives of South Africa, because they are supposed to be the children of Ham, are by this prophecy condemned to eternal servitude, has no foundation in Scripture' (op. cit., p. 114).

9.3 Conclusion

The notion that the differentiation of the human race would originally have occurred only within the family relationship, is only valid for the state of perfection before the Fall. One may assume that if from the outset man had moved to all corners of the earth in accordance with the command God at the creation of man, geographic, climatological and other circumstances would undoubtedly have enhanced the process of differentiation in terms of biological, cultural and political differences. The fundamental difference between believers and non-believers would also have played a major role in this process, if it had not been for the fact that the two groups had become intermixed, to the disadvantage of the believers (Gen. 6). In the light of this we must therefore assume that differentiation of 'peoples' is implicit in the command of the creation and that the events at Babel merely gave it a new momentum and character. The data in Gen. 10 and 11 eradicate all heathenish ethnocentrism and unfounded cosmopolitanism. The diversity of peoples is rooted in the primary unity of the human race and in the fact that all peoples are fundamentally equal in their responsibility and relationship to God. At the same time we intend to show in these chapters that the development of the human race in organic-social contexts is also the will of God for this dispensation. Therefore we emphasise 'families', 'nations' and 'countries', with 'language' as an important distinguishing factor.

In the normative consideration of the Bible, the negative element lies not so much in the diversity of peoples as such, but rather in the disruption and disharmony as a result of sin and broken communication. The Scriptural solution for these disrupted relationships is not a humanistic attempt at unity based on the arrogance of man (Babel!), but lies in the unity of the blessing which God promised to and through Abraham and which man had to search for (Acts 17 : 27).

The calling of Abraham and the life of the chosen people should be seen against the background of the cultural situation of the Near East in those times, which was characterised by a relatively unitary culture and by population migrations and admixtures on a fairly large scale. In Biblical times, the Near East was marked by an open situation in respect of inter-race and inter-people relationships, and in respect of cultural cross-fertilisation.

An entirely new situation arose with the calling of Abraham. It was no longer a matter of ethnic diversity as such, but rather of the distinction between Israel and the other nations. As the Dutch Study Commission rightly points out, 'Israel is, as it were, lifted from among the nations, to be set apart'. This process did not, however, take place in a cultural-historical void. Both the patriarchs and the Israelite people came into contact with the ethnic diversity and the cultural situation of those times at every stage of their eventful and stirring history. The story of the Bible reflects this contact, however indirectly.

The conclusion to which this investigation leads us is that in biblical times the situation in the Near East was open and dynamic, in respect of both ethnicity and culture. Owing to the network of trade routes, the wide reach of some of the languages, and the continuous migration of certain groups, including national migrations on an unprecedented scale, there was a steady and persistent exchange of cultural values, even an intermixture of people. The cultural and biological intermixture was not always limited to the same race, as evidenced by the "racial situation" as reflected in Palestine. The data in the Old Testament regarding Israel and the nations must be considered against this cultural-historical background.

10. Israel and the nations

In order to acquire a true insight into the new situation which arose in revelation history with the calling of Abraham and the separation of Israel, it is necessary to consider the distinctive ethos of Israel and its unique relationship to the heathen nations. The holy command that Israel should continue to exist independently vis-à-vis the other peoples,

cannot be applied directly, but certainly by way of analogy, to the situation of the present day. In the case of Israel the multinational demand for isolation was motivated primarily by religious and not by racial or ethnic considerations. Even if we were to admit that Israel's existence had ethnic significance as well, this aspect cannot be isolated from Israel's unique position as the chosen people of God and it would therefore be inadvisable for the church to draw unwarranted conclusions from it to be applied to relations between the peoples of our times. There were more than mere ethnic or political factors at stake in the heathen nations' conduct towards Israel and cognisance should be taken of the salvation-historical premise which in this instance is revealed in the antithesis between the kingdom of the world and that of God.

The calling of Abraham is a turning-point in the history of God's concern for the world and, therefore, also for the nations of the world. The Dutch Study Commission puts it as follows; "Abraham is called away from Ur and Israel is isolated as a people so that God's plan of salvation for the nations may be realised." We also agree with the following explanation. "As early as the chapter immediately following on the one in which the building of the tower of Babel is described, we are told how, at God's bidding, Abraham had to leave his country and say farewell to his family. In the evocative words of Gen. 12 : 1, he had to leave the house (bayith, oikos) of his father to found a new house on the basis of faith and obedience to his God and Father in heaven (Gen. 15 : 6). Subsequently, God makes a convenant with Abraham and his house (Gen. 17 : 12, 13). Thus this patriarch is isolated as the bearer of God's blessed promise. As blessed one he will be a blessing for the entire world. In the history of the patriarchs it is repeated five times that all generations of the earth will be blessed with Abraham and his family (thrice to Abraham: Gen. 12 : 3, 18 : 8 and 22 : 18; once to Isaac: Gen. 25 : 4, and once to Jacob: Gen. 28 : 14)". The Commission rightly adds: "The people descended from Abraham – and in what a wonderful fashion! – must bear the promise and the treasure of salvation throughout the ages until the final fulfilment in Christ."

In considering inter-race and inter-people relations in the light of Scripture, cognisance must be taken of the unique position occupied by Israel, the chosen people of God, among the nations of that time. The holy command that Israel should continue to exist independently vis-à-vis the other people, cannot be applied directly, but certainly by way of analogy, to the present-day ethnic situation. In the case of Israel the demand for isolation has a significance for the history of salvation and cannot be directly applied to the population situation

22

of our own time. Even if we should acknowledge that Israel's existence also had an ethnic significance, this aspect cannot be divorced from its unique position as chosen people of God and it is therefore not advisable for the church to draw any unwarranted conclusions from this, nor to apply them to the population situation of our times.

In the social differentiation within Israel's national community, the position of the stranger was typical of the mutual relationships of that time: on the one hand, his social position was not in all respects as favourable as that of the true Israelite; and, on the other hand, social intercourse among the peoples was fairly free. In everyday life there was no separation or segregation between the stranger and the true Israelite. In considering this open situation in the national relationships in Israel, we must also take into account the fact that there was a large measure of cultural and racial equality in the Near East of those times. It is possibly due to this fact that the Bible knows no racial problem, even in respect of the position of the stranger.

For the purposes of our study it is important to note that the Old Testament fully accepts the reality of the existence of nations and peoples. There is no question of Western dualism and spiritualism in considering and evaluating the geographic and national aspects of the existence of the peoples concerned. Although Deut. 32 : 8 has no firm interpretation (the text is subject to dispute), it nevertheless seems to indicate that the fate of people is not beyond the will and intervention of God: on occasion He even assigned each its own homeland (cf. also Amos 9 : 7). On the other hand, the Old Testament is also clear on the point that no people or culture is an inviolable entity. Peoples came and went and in some instances they were even destroyed at the bidding of God (the Canaanites). No people was allowed, for instance, to act entirely at its own discretion in determining its relations with other peoples. God also dispensed his international law outside Israel. A typical example is given in Amos 2 : 1-3 where Moab is judged because he had incinerated the bones of the king of Edom. The mutilation of corpses by fire was a serious offence in the East in those days (cf. Isaiah 33 : 12; 2 Kings 23 : 16). This judgment shows that the moral injunctions of God also apply to peoples other than the Israelites. The Old Testament knows (and censures) the arrogance (hybris) of nations and particularly of their rulers (cf. Isaiah 10 : 7, Hab. 1 : 12-17), but at the same time there is no mention in the Old Testament of peoples or races inherently superior or inferior (cf. Eichrodt: **Das Menschenverständnis des A.T.**, p. 35). It is true that the nations were in a sense outside the scope of the revelation of God (cf. Ps. 147 : 19, 20; Acts 14 : 16; 17 : 30), but this did not mean that He did not concern himself with them at all: they were also objects of his judgment and salvation.

Any analogy between the situation regarding Israel and the nations, on the one hand, and inter-group relationship of today, on the other, should be drawn with a good deal of caution. In this regard, H. du Plessis warns that the chosen people had a unique calling and therefore we cannot today justify racial apartheid and discrimination on the basis of the distinction which Israel had to maintain (op. cit. p. 53). There were more than mere ethnic or political factors involved in the conduct of the heathen nations towards Israel and one should at all times take into account the salvation-historical factor of viewpoint which, in this instance, is revealed in the antithesis between the kingdom of the earth and that of God.

The word "stranger" is deliberately used in quotation marks because we have to take into account various distinctions. In the first place, the word "stranger" is in many instances applied to Israel itself or to individual Israelites, so that it does not always refer to other population groups (cf. i.a. Gen. 23 : 4; Ex. 2 : 22; 18 : 3; 22 : 20; 23 : 9; Deut. 10 : 19; 23 : 8; Judges 17 : 7-9; 19 : 1, 6; Ruth 1 : 1; 2 Sam. 4 : 3, etc.).

Secondly, the true "strangers" who sojourned in Israel for longer or shorter periods were not all of the same category. We may distinguish the "foreigners in transit" who were indeed given hospitality but in some respects were not protected by law (cf. Deut. 15 : 3; 23 : 20; both texts concern the **nokri),** and the "residential foreigners", more particularly the so-called **gerîm.**

It is evident that, apart from a few restrictive measures, there was a relatively free intercourse in the inter-people relationships in Israel. This generous treatment of "strangers" within the gates of Israel was probably inspired by the following motives: the historical consideration that the Israelites had once been strangers in Egypt (Ex. 6 : 3; Lev. 19 : 34; Deut. 10 : 18-19; 23 : 7); the moral requirement that charity should be shown to all (Lev. 19 : 10; 23 : 22; Deut. 10 : 18; 24 : 19-21; Ps. 146 : 9; Mal. 3 : 5) and neighbourly love (Lev. 19 : 34; Deut. 10 : 19), and the fact that the strangers had joined the ranks of the faithful (Isaiah 56 : 3, 6, in which texts mention is made of the **bené hannekar,** or sons of the stranger; cf. also Ex. 12 : 48, 49). Racial considerations obviously played no significant role in this intercourse (cf. Deut. 23 : 3, 8). While it is true that the racial identity of the foreign "strangers" cannot always be established with any certainty, it would, however, be mere speculation to state that the strangers concerned were at all times of the same "race" as the Israelites. Texts such as Ex. 12 : 38, Lev.

24 : 10, Num 11 : 4, Deut. 23 : 3 and 8, Ezek. 20 : 5-10, Amos 5 : 25, 26, Neh 13 : 3 and others should prevent us from arriving at too hasty a conclusion in this respect. We may safely assume that most of the foreign "strangers" were indeed members of the Semitic "race", but it is at the same time clear that they also included members of other "races".

In considering these data, we must take account of the fact that there was a large measure of racial and cultural equality in the Near East in those times. It is probably also due to this fact that there is no mention in the Bible of a racial **problem** in respect of the position of the "strangers". The spirit of exclusivism prevalent among the Israelites in this regard should be attributed to other facors, rather than to any consciousness of racial identity. Such factors were the religious fervour which flowed from the fact that they were the chosen people of God, and a certain xenophobia which the Israelites shared with other nations in the area, especially the Egyptians. It is nevertheless a fact that ethnic considerations played no significant role in deciding who should be excluded from the "kehal Jahwe" (cf. J. D. W. Kritzinger: **Qehal Jahwe**, p. 145, and Koole, op cit., in **Schrift en Uitleg**, p. 83).

11. Emphases in the teaching of the Old Testament

In the teaching of the Old Testament on the subject of the existence and mutual relationships of peoples, the theological, salvation-historical and corporative viewpoints are of decisive significance, while special attention should be accorded to cardinal concepts such as charity, justice, truth and peace which are the fundamental tenets of the Biblical message. In considering relationships between races and peoples, account should always be taken of the fact that the peoples comprise individuals created in the image of God, and that He will call all peoples to account for their conduct towards other peoples.

This theocentric alignment to God of all people and all peoples is not merely based on the fact of God's creation and leadership in history, but it is also aligned to the history of salvation. The latter premise is of the utmost importance to the church. It is the most important function of the church to impart to all people and peoples the salvation which has become a reality in Christ. This also presupposes that the church will watch over relationships, structures and situations which may be an obstacle to the progress of the gospel. Moreover, it is characteristic of the message of the Old Testament that the individual is corporately included in the various community associations to which he belongs. This premise is also of importance to the church. On the one hand, it means that the church must exert itself to give concrete substance to the blessings of the gospel in the life and social structure of a people. On the other hand, the church should avoid the modern tendency to erase all distinctions among peoples. The rich significance of some of the cardinal concepts of the Old Testament clearly indicates that in the mutual relationships between races and peoples, LOVE is also the fulfilment of the law, that JUSTICE is a basic concept in the determination of such relationships, that the problems arising from relationships between races and peoples cannot be solved unless the TRUTH prevails in its full significance, and unless there is PEACE, in the sense of the stabilisation of all relationships and as the result of the atonement of the Prince of Peace.

The teachings of the Old Testament particularly deal with certain fundamental concepts which may assist us better to understand the normative character of all relationships between people, and therefore between peoples. We would like to draw the attention to the concepts love, justice, truth and peace.

Love ('ahab) of God and one's neighbour is not only the summary of the law in the New Testament (Matthew 22 : 37-40), but also of that of the Old Testament. Because its Lord God is an only God, Israel must love its Lord God fully and completely (Deut. 6 : 5). The same theocentric motivation is given for neighbourly love. "Thou shalt not avenge, nor bear any grudge against the children of thy people, but thou shalt love thy neighbour as thyself: I am the LORD" (Lev. 19 : 18). This mandate does not, however, apply only to the "children of thy people". "But the stranger that dwelleth with you shall be unto you as one born among you, and thou shalt love him as thyself . . . I am the LORD your GOD" (Lev. 19 : 34). Love is the consummation of the law also in the relationships among races and peoples.

Justice is a complicated concept: it refers to the message of salvation, the accomplishment of redemption, but also to the mandate of punishment. In the mutual relations of individuals and peoples, it refers particularly to doing what is right, to let justice be done. The words of the author of Proverbs are applicable here: "Righteousness (sedakâ) exalteth a nation (gôi); but sin is a reproach to any people" (14 : 34). The prophetic preaching is concerned mainly with the maintenace of law and justice at both the social and international level. Justice is a basic concept in the determination of relations between peoples and nations.

The word for **truth** ('emet) is derived from the same root as the word "amen" which actually means "to stand fast". Where there is "truth", there is strength. The firmness or strength of "truth" is revealed in various concrete ways, in the sense of stability (2 Kings

20 : 19, Isaiah 39 : 8), but also genuineness, veracity, as opposed to appearances which deceive (Proverbs 11 : 18; Isaiah 2 : 21, 10 : 10); sincerity and honesty, as opposed to hypocrisy and duplicity (Ps. 51 : 8; Proverbs 12 : 19); when it refers to jurisprudence the word 'emet means justice and righteousness (Zech. 7 : 9; 8 : 16, 19). It is often translated by the words "faith" and "royalty" – to indicate that way of life in which a person does not hesitate to fulfil his obligations (Ps. 31 : 6; 146 : 6). The word 'emet is often used to indicate that something that has been said, is in accordance with the facts. In this sense it is the opposite of "lie" or "error" and is translated by the word "truth" (Gen. 42 : 16; 1 Kings 10 : 6).

Thus the word **"truth"** has a comprehensive meaning in the Old Testament. Truth is violated when in a society deceitful appearances are kept up, hypocrisy and deceit are the order of the day, when there is no longer justice and righteousness, faith is lacking and people can no longer be taken at their word. When "truth falls in the street" (Isaiah 59 : 14), everything that gives stability to life falls with it.

Few concepts of the Old Testament are so directly applicable to our times as the concept "truth". Is it not part of our dilemma that the ever shrinking world does not lead to greater understanding and insight and consequently to better relationships, but is, on the contrary, plagued by broken communications on all fronts, by misconceptions and misunderstandings and malicious distortion of facts? In this respect the communication media (press, radio and television) are often the instruments of the "trouble and evil" which beset the nations of the present world. The problems of racial and inter-people relations cannot be solved unless justice is done to "truth" in the fullest and richest sense of the word.

The last word that we have to deal with is **peace** (Shalom). This word is as rich in meaning as all the others.

Basically the word means "welfare" or well-being. The condition of "well-being" arises from stabilised religious, political and social relationships. If these relationships are disturbed, there can be no "peace". Peace is something experienced by the individual, but more particularly, by a people as "well-being" in the political, social and religious context. "Shalom is something seen in the fruit of labour and in the manner in which people have social intercourse with one another. Righteousness and peace kiss one another, according to Psalm 85 : 11. Shalom is not a feeling but a condition in which ordinary life is led. There is something tangible to it; man experiences it with his whole existence, his body and soul. Thus the opposite of peace in the Old Testament is not necessarily war but

rather catastrophe, unhappiness, strife, misery and, of course, war"
(F. J. Pop: **Bijbelse woorden en hun geheim**, s.v.: "vrede").

True peace is a gift of the blessing of God (Numbers 6 : 20), and
eventually the fruit of the actions of the Prince of Peace (Isaiah
9 : 5). Nowadays there is a need for the preaching of this "peace",
in the sense of the stabilisation of all relationships, including those
between races and peoples, but in such a way that it is borne from
inside by the fruit of the atonement of the Prince of Peace. There is
also a "Pax Romana", a secular peace, a "peace" enforced from
outside and above, which employs violence (arms, intimidation,
boycotts) to force people into line. There is no essential need for
this kind of "peace", for it does not stabilise relationships. On the
contrary, it destroys them.

These few references make it clear that the teaching of the Old
Testament is rich and topical, also for the existence of the nations in
their inter-relationships. It is the function of the church to bring
God's entire message to the people of our age.

SCRIPTURAL DATA: NEW TESTAMENT

**12. What has been said in para. 2 on the Word of God as a point of
departure also applies to the New Testament.**

**12.1 The modern scientific distinction between the concepts "people",
'nation", "population" and "ethnos" are not known in the New
Testament, which does not specifically deal with the concept
"race" either.**

The Greek words **ethnos** and **laos** do not specifically denote to our
distinction between "people" and "nation", but we may nevertheless
assume that these two Greek words are closest in meaning to our
modern usage of "people" as a unit characterised and conjoined by
a common language and culture (cf. e.g. Acts 2 : 5).

In the Afrikaans translation of the Bible **laos** is usually rendered as
"people" and **ethnos** as "nation", but does not intend to make a
ethnological distinction. (The possible explanation is to be found in
the fact that **laos** is usually used for the people of God while **ethnos**
signifies the heathen nations.) In this publication we use the word
"people" as a rule, because it covers both concepts **laos** and **ethnos**
effectively. Where the Afrikaans translation of the Bible is quoted
we use the original word in the text.

In the New Testament there is no reference to the concept "race".
Even where reference to a person's racial identity might have been
relevant, as in the case of Simon the Cyrenian (St. Mark 15 : 21),

the eunuch of Ethiopia (Acts 8 : 27) and Simeon Niger (Acts 13 :1), some of whom might have been members of the Negroid race, no special attention is paid to the racial aspect. For this reason we use the term "national" or "inter-people relations" in this report.

12.2 For an understanding of the teachings of the New Testament on the subject of national relations, a survey of the cultural-historical situation of that time is instructive.
Christianity appeared on the world scene in one of the most interesting phases in history. For several reasons it is imperative to have some understanding of the circumstances in which the gospel was heard and had to make its influence felt. The principles derived from this confrontation between the gospel and the world are valid and decisive for all times.
Christianity appeared on the scene and the gospel was preached for the first time in a world comprising various peoples and races living within one Roman Empire but with a variety of political, social and religious structures. The important question is how Paul reacted to this situation and to these interrelationships. In several letters Paul emphasises the fact that as a result of the coming of Christ and the redemption accomplished by Him, the distinction between Israel and the nations which existed in the time of the Old Testament now belonged to the past. In the new dispensation, national, cultural, social and biological factors (which will always be there, of course) had acquired a new unity in Christ (Gal. 3 : 28; Col. 3 : 11). We have all been baptised by one Spirit into one body – Jew, Greek, slave and freeman – and we have all "been made to drink of one Spirit" (1 Cor. 12 : 13).
Although there is a diversity of members in the church as in the body of man, there is nevertheless a unity in the diversity (1 Cor. 12). In Asia Minor, and particularly in Corinth, with its large variety of races and people, the message was to be heard that, despite the differences among them, God gave them the opportunity to share in one great common task, the expansion of His kingdom on earth. As peoples (nations) they had the right to an independent existence and survival, but their mutual relationships had to be determined by this common objective and the all-prevailing principle within the kingdom – the love for God and one another.

13. The teaching of the New Testament on the question of national relationships in the general social field.

13.1 The new Testament upholds the equivalence of all people and nations.

That the New Testament accepts the basic equivalence (equal value) of all people and of all peoples and nations can be demonstrated from various premises. Of the many New Testament guidelines in this respect we shall mention only the following:

The nations are all descended from one (man), i.e. Adam (Acts 17 : 26). The reading "of one blood" is less likely, but is basically the same concept.

The Old Testament teaching that man was created in the image of God is not explicitly enlarged upon but it is assumed throughout: cf. 1 Cor. 11 : 7, Col. 3 : 10; Eph. 4 : 24. (Also consult H. Ridderbos: **Paulus, ontwerp van zijn theologie,** p. 70 et seq. 246, et seq.). There is unfortunately no unanimity on the interpretation of Hebr. 2 : 6-8, but many interpreters, including Grosheide, consider this to be a description of the glory, honour, sovereignty and responsibility which God had granted man and which will be restored completely in the fullness of time.

The New Testament emphasises the fact that all people are living under sin (Romans 3 : 9 et seq., 23; 5 : 12; Eph. 2 : 3, etc).

With his incarnation Christ assumed a human body, became flesh, i.e. He participated in our entire human existence in its broken reality (St. John 1 : 14; cf. Hebr. 2 : 14 et seq.).

Salvation in Christ is offered of all peoples and nations, without any distinction whatsoever (St. Matthew 28 : 19; St. John 3 : 16; Acts 1 : 8; 2 : 5; Romans 3 : 22; cf. Ham and Canaan in the Old Testament).

The glory of the **eschaton** is the destiny of the believers from all nations (Revelations 21 : 24, 26; 22 : 2. For the present era also see Revelations 5 : 9; 7 : 9).

13.2. The New Testament maintains the unity and solidarity of the human race.

All the premises mentioned under proposition I also emphasise the unity and solidarity of the human race. The human race is bound together by a common descent, the fall of man, the universal offer of grace and the eshatological destination.

13.3 The commandment of neighbourly love is based on the injunction of God, but is at the same time related to the equivalence, unity and solidarity of all peoples.

The commandment "Love thy neighbour as thyself", which in the New Testament takes precedence as the decisive norm for all personal and social relationships (Matt. 22 : 39 – see also proposition 8 below) is not based on the dignity of man as such or on the solidarity of the human race, but solely on the injunction of God. From the point of view of man, the significance of this commandment lies in the fact that man can be commanded to love his neighbour as himself because all people are equivalent, and in the fact that it interprets the solidarity of the human race in terms of a reliance on and a responsibility for one another in love.

13.4 The New Testament accepts and upholds the fact of the diversity of peoples.

The New Testament does not question or abrogate the equivalence and solidarity of peoples. At the same time it accepts the fact of the existence of a diversity of peoples (Matt. 28 : 19; Acts 2 : 5; Rom. 1 : 16, etc.). Moreover, in Acts 17 : 26 reference is made to the fact that God appointed specific times for the various nations as well as boundaries for their homelands. These parts should, however, be read in the context of the message of the New Testament – the teaching of the coming of the kingdom of God, and one should be careful not to read facts into these verses which fall outside their scope. It would not be permissible to infer from these verses a Scriptural justification for the separate development of all peoples under all circumstances. Revelation 21 : 24, 26 is also of importance in this regard. These verses state not only that the "nations" will share in the new Jerusalem, but also that the "glory and honour" of the kings and nations will be brought into Jerusalem.

One may ask whether this is not a reference to the multiplicity of cultural and other treasures with which the nations in their diversity will enrich the new dispensation to the glory of God. Thus it is a distinct possibility that we have here a marked emphasis on the special value of the diversity of nations in the overall plan of God. One has to admit, however, that there is no unanimity as to the exact interpretation of these verses and that the final word on them has not yet been spoken. What is of more significance, is the fact that the New Testament often refers to the diversity of nations but never characterises it as sinful; nor does it ever call upon Christians to renounce their nationality. Paul makes no apology for the fact that he is a Jew; nor does he consider it his Christian duty to deny this fact (Rom. 16 : 7, 11; 11 : 1; Phil. 3 : 5). In spite of his regard for all other peoples, he loves his own people so passionately that he grieves for their lack of faith and declares himself ready to be "anathema from Christ, for my brethren's sake, my kinsmen according to the flesh" (Rom. 9 : 3). Even apart from what is stated in

Revelations 21, we may therefore assent that the diversity of nations, coupled with a sound commitment to one's own nation, is not considered sinful in the new Testament: on the contrary, it is accepted as a factual, even a positive, proposition.

13.5 The New Testament accepts the diversity of peoples as a fact, but does not elevate it to the only or highest principle.

That the New Testament accepts the diversity of peoples but does not elevate it to the only or highest principle, is emphatically stated in a passage such as Gal. 3 : 28: "There can be neither Jew nor Greek, there can be neither bond nor free, there can be no male and female: for ye all are one in Christ Jesus". The differences in national relations, social position and sex are not annulled (for the visible church) – that would be absurd – but they are transcended and sanctified by the tremendous fact of the new unity in Christ. The diversity survives but has only a relative significance before the great miracle of the new life in Christ. The same applies to Col. 3 : 11. To read into these passages a mandate for social integration between peoples would be to abuse them. It is obviously the purpose of these verses to emphasise the all-prevailing importance of the new unity in Christ but not to deny the existence of individual and diverse communities.

13.6 In specific circumstances and under specific conditions the New Testament makes provision for the regulation on the basis of separate development of the co-existence of various peoples in one country.

From the fact that the existence of a diversity of peoples is accepted as a relative, but nevertheless real, premise, one may infer that the New Testament allows for the possibility that a given country may decide to regulate its inter-people relationships on the basis of separate development – considering its own peculiar circumstances, with due respect for the basic norms which the Bible prescribes for the regulation of social relations (cf. proposition 3.2.8) and after careful consideration of all possible solutions offered. When such a country honestly comes to the conclusion that the ethical norms for ordering social relationships, i.e. love of one's neighbour and social justice, can best be realized on the basis of parallel development, and if such a conviction is based on factual reasoning, the choice of parallel development can be justified in the light of what the Bible teaches (RES, Grand Rapids, p. 32 and 225, RES Lunteren, p. 340 and RES, Sydney, p. 330).

13.7 According to the New Testament, the danger of a sinful separation of peoples is ever present in the diversity of peoples. The church of Jesus Christ should at all times take cognisance of those situations which may promote estrangement and must do everything in its power to establish mutual understanding and respect, to talk over problems and to build bridges which will prevent the diversity from becoming a sinful spiritual estrangement.

The New Testament not only accepts the diversity of nations but also teaches us how easily the sinful nature of man can lead to spiritual estrangement, illusions of superiority, exploitation, suspicion, hatred and enmity among peoples. The New Testament recounts the tension between Jew and Samaritan which assumed such proportions that it was not even permissible to offer one another a drink of water (John 4 : 9, cf. also Luke 10 : 33); of the attitude of superiority which Romans adopted towards Jews (Mark 15 : 9 et seq., cf. John 18 : 36); of the prejudice and egotism of the Christian Jew who would not deign to dine with Christians from the heathen world (Gal. 2 : 11 et seq.). We also learn that one of the most serious problems faced by the first congregation was due to the discrimination practiced by the Aramic-speaking Christians against the widows of the Greek-speaking (Acts 6 : 1). If it is true that people in their sinful state are hateful and hate one another (Titus 3 : 3), attitudes of hostility between various groups and peoples are much more probable because the likelihood of a group reaction is so much greater. The church of Jesus Christ and the various nations must at all times take into account these possibilities for estrangement and must do everything in their power to encourage mutual understanding and respect, to talk over problems and to build bridges which will prevent the diversity from becoming a sinful spiritual estrangement. The church must be on its guard against and caution against selfishness among peoples and their tendency to be concerned only with their own interests at the expense of those of other peoples, since this renders them apathetic and shortsighted in respect of the needs of other peoples.

13.8 The commandment "love thy neighbour as thyself" is the ethical norm for the regulation of relationships among peoples.

We have already pointed out that love for one's neighbour as ethical norm for the regulation of relations among peoples is related to the equality and solidarity of peoples. We must now consider love for one's neighbour as guide-line for behaviour between groups and peoples. In the New Testament this commandment is given within the context of individual ethics: one should love one's neighbour as oneself. (It is significant that Jesus elucidates this commandment in the light of the meeting of people from disparate population groups, i.e. Jew and Samaritan – Luke 10 : 29, et seq.). However, it is exegetically permissible to project the line from individual ethics to relationships between groups and peoples. As is abundantly evident from Jesus' actions and behaviour in the New Testament, this neighbourly love is no weak, sentimental love, but a love that acts; it is a love which does not wish to transform the neighbour into a replica of oneself but accepts him in his own right as someone created in the image of God and accords him sufficient scope for true self-realisation. The concrete manifestation of this neighbourly love obviously varies according to circumstances. It can take the form of a practical offer of help in an hour of need (Luke 10 : 30 et seq., Matt. 25 : 35 et seq., James 2 : 15-16); of help by the strong in bearing the infirmities of the weak (Romans 15 : 1-2); friendship, benificence and hospitality (Phil. 5 : 4; Gal. 6 : 10; Romans 12 : 13; Hebr. 13 : 2). This should occur in the disposition described in passages such as Philip. 2 : 1-8. The full meaning of the commandment of neighbourly love is particularly well elucidated in the "golden rule": "All things therefore what-soever ye would that men should do unto you, even so do ye also unto them." At its very least the application of the commandment of love for one's neighbour implies social justice (cf. Matthew 23 : 23). When applied to relationships between peoples, this demand for social justice means that any one people will grant to others the same rights and privileges which it demands for itself. Where a people has been temporarily placed in a position where it governs the fortunes of another people or peoples, it must at all times check its actions against this demand for justice and, in particular, it must carefully guard against self-aggrandisement at the expense of others (Romans 15 : 1 (b) cf. Philip. 2 : 3, 4). This demand for social justice applies to all aspects of relationships between peoples, as well as of the relationship between master and servant: "Masters, render unto your servants that which is just and equal; knowing that ye also have a Master in heaven" (Col. 4 : 1). Social justice in New Testament terms would therefore also include such practical measures as fair wages and decent working conditions.

The life and viability of man and of a people is a gift of God which should be protected and treated with a sense of responsibility (cf. e.g. Paul who consistently states his case in front of the authorities concerned). It is therefore perfectly permissible within the context of the second commandment for a person or his people to protect or

34

safeguard their own life or existence, **provided the interests of others are not sacrificed to self-interest** (cf. RES, Lutheren, p. 340 and RES, Sydney, p. 330).

13.9 The commandment of neighbourly love must also find expression in justice.

In the Bible the concept justice is used both in respect of God's relationship to man (Romans 1 : 17, 3 : 21) and the relationships between people (Matthew 20 : 1, et seq., Matthew 5 : 20). God's justice is the sum total of His acts through which He fulfilled His promises to the peoples of Israel in the Old Testament and through which in the New Testament He redeemed His church and placed it in the service of His Kingdom. And he who accepts God's acts in Jesus Christ, has been made just, for in meeting the demands of law, Christ acquired justice for all those who believe in Him (1 Cor. 1 : 30; 2 Cor. 5 : 21). Thus, in God justice and mercy are one.

Justice in interpersonal relations is generally grounded in the law-abiding acts of one person towards another. Thus justice demands in the first place acts of love towards every person, regardless of his status, descent and culture. In this sense every man must receive the same, namely love.

But Scriptural justice is not merely based on the equivalence of all peoples as created in the image of God; it also takes cognisance of the inequality of gifts and talents, circumstances and responsibilities of each person, for these also come from God (Matthew 25 : 14, et seq.). In this sense all people are not given the same.

Justice is therefore those acts in which man receives that which God decrees to him in his peculiar circumstances and with which he is expected to fulfil his divine calling as a human being. The various forms in which justice is done to the individual or the group are not static or immutable: they are dynamic and will vary from situation to situation. In each given situation, however, the ideal is the greatest possible measure of justice commensurate with the circumstances.

Those who believe in God, in particular, are called upon to show justice in abundance in that they must give more to others because the love of Christ has been shed in their hearts (Romans 5 : 5) and because they follow his example (Matthew 5 : 43-48; Romans 15 : 1, 2, 7; 2 Cor. 8 : 8-9; Philip. 2 : 3-8).

13.10 It is the calling of the church to exhort its members, the authorities and subjects to uphold the ethical principles which must be applied in the regulation of inter-people relationships.

In respect of inter-people relationships, church and people are confronted with the demand in the New Testament of love for one's neighbour, and in particular to act in absolute justice. The church realises that this justice will be an absolute reality only in the **eschaton** (the fullness of time) when justice will reign on the new earth (2 Peter 3 : 13). In the light of Scripture the church also knows in how imperfect a manner this demand is being fulfilled on this side of eternity. Thus the church is faced with a double temptation. It may eliminate the tension between the present and the **eschaton** by throwing in the towel or by suppressing the ethical imperative out of fear and by consoling itself in the prospect that everything will be different in the **eschaton.** But this would amount to neglect of duty. It is the function of the church to preach to the state, the citizens of the state and to its members the great Scriptural principles which have to be adhered to in human relationships, so that signs of the **eschaton** may be established even in the present era.

The second temptation with which the church is confronted is a desire to eliminate the conflict between the present and the **eschaton** by trying to enforce the latter without due regard for the complexity of the concrete situation. While it guards, on the one hand, against a false and sinful acquiescence in the **status quo** and, on the other hand, against an unrealistic enforcement of the **eschaton,** the church must nevertheless continue to bring its prophetic message so that the supremacy of God may become apparent in all spheres of life.

14. The testimony of the New Testament on inter-people relationships within the Church of Christ.

14.1 In contrast to the case of the people of God in the Old Testament, the church of Jesus Christ transcends all cultic dispensations, as embodied in the ceremonial laws, as well as all geographical and national boundaries which were applicable under the old dispensation.

The New Testament sees the church as, inter alia, the people of God (Acts 15 : 14; Romans 9 : 25; 2 Cor. 6 : 16; Titus 2 : 14; Hebr. 4 : 9; 8 : 10; 1 Peter 2 : 9-10). Its origin and survival are not the result of the natural process of propagation and growth, but of God's merciful and faithful providence in its calling on the basis of the atonement of Jesus Christ. Membership of this "people of God" is not debarred by the separation between Jew and heathen (Eph.

2 : 14), but is acquired on the basis of belief in Jesus Christ (Gal. 3 : 28). The term "people of God" in this way acquires a purely religious connotation which is not determined by biological, cultural, national and other factors (Gal. 3 : 28, Col. 3 : 11).

14.2 The unity of the church is a unity in Christ. It is a community of faith which transcends all divisions.

The point of departure of the New Testament is the unity of the church in Jesus Christ. The church is the manifestation of one people, one bride, one flock, one temple of God and one body of Christ (cf. 1 Cor. 10 : 17, 1 Cor. 12 : 12; Eph. 2 : 16). They are one owing to the fact that there is but one Lord, one faith, one baptism, one God and Father of all (Eph. 4 : 4-6). This unity is in the first place a confessional reality of faith in Christ, but at the same time it should be experienced and applied according to circumstances and the concrete realities of the church's existence (cf. John. 17 : 21; 1 Cor. 1 : 12, 4 : 6; Eph. 2 : 14). The norm for this unity was given in Christ and is determined by the truth of the gospel (cf. John 17 : 6-17).

14.3 The New Testament makes an important distinction between the universal and the local church.

In the New Testament we learn about both a universal and a local church. This church is the body of Christ (Eph. 1 : 10; 2 : 16; 3 : 6; Col. 1 : 18). The universal church comprises all people as they are gathered together by the gospel (Col. 1 : 23). The church is in fact humanity redeemed in Christ, the second Adam (Rom. 5 : 12-18; 1 Cor. 15 : 45). The local church is the local congregation or church – in a geographic sense. Each local church is a revelation of the body of Christ at that particular place.

14.4 Although there is no multiplicity of churches in the New Testament, there may be some considerations on which a grouping in various "churches" may be justified. When in the New Testament mention is made of variety in the church, it is always a variety within one church. The unity of the church is therefore always of primary importance.

The New Testament does not recognise a multiplicity of churches, in view of the presupposition of the unity of the church of Christ. And yet one may infer that there can be a possibility of diversity within the one church of Jesus Christ. Paul speaks of the congregations (or churches) of Galatia (1 Cor. 16 : 1; Gal. 1 : 21), of Asia (1 Cor. 16 : 19), of Macedonia (2 Cor. 8 : 1), of Judea (Gal. 1 : 22), of Syria and Cilicia (Acts 15 : 41), of all the congregations of the heathens (Romans 16 : 5), of the congregations of Christ (Romans 16 : 16). It is therefore possible that each of these churches also had its own emphasis in the formulation of its creed or confession and its own typical structure in accordance with its own particular cultural milieu. The most significant point, however, is that this diversity does not abrogate unity. We have here a diversity within one church.

14.5 The natural diversity of people and nations continues to exist in the church of Christ, but is sanctified in Him.

One may not infer from the New Testament that the natural diversity of people and nations is abrogated by the new unity of faith in Christ. (Matthew 28 : 19) Jesus commanded the disciples to proclaim the gospel among the nations, following on the promise to Abraham (Gen. 12 : 3; 22 : 18). Revelations 21 : 24 is very clear on this point: "And the nations of those that are saved shall walk amidst the light thereof", i.e. in the light of God and of the Lamb. These natural relationships are, however, sanctified in Christ by the gospel and they may not degenerate into a glorification of the self at the expense of others.

14.6 Diversity in the church may never lead to spiritual estrangement. Thus the most serious attention must at all times be given to the New Testament concepts of the brotherhood in Christ and of the koinonia.

While the New Testament teaches the unity of the church as well as diversity within the unity, there is always the urgent imperative of the gospel that all are mutually responsible for one another in the church of Jesus Christ. The brotherly love for one another of which 1 John 4 : 11 speaks and which the whole letter of John extols so eloquently (cf. John 2 : 9-11, also Romans 12 : 10; 1 Thess. 4 : 9; Hebr. 13 : 1; 1 Peter 1 : 22; 2 Peter 1 : 7), the willingness with which we must render service to one another (John 13 : 14) and the fellowship to which we are called in the body of Christ together with the faithful, in order mutually to care for one another (1 Cor. 12 : 25, cf. Romans 15 : 1; 1 Cor. 8 : 7 et seq.) – all these must continually be practised and manifested in the church. This is all the more necessary because linguistic, cultural and other differences may easily lead to tensions, misunderstandings and spiritual estrangement (cf. Acts. 6 : 1; Romans 15 : 5 et seq.). How these requirements should manifest themselves in the practice of the institutionalised church, cannot be argued in the abstract but are to be determined by the practical realities of the human situations in which, in the imperfect now, the church finds itself.

Chapter 2

The Church, the Kingdom and the Oikomene

15. All reflections on the church should proceed from the perspective of the kingdom of God and in submission to the theocentric principle.

A clear picture of the **church,** its being, task, calling and limitation can only be obtained when considered in the light of God's total plan with the whole of creation. God's actions form one organic whole: thus the church ought not to be considered or evaluated as an isolated or independent entity. If we should seek a concept which comprises **all** God's acts, which reveals the deepest significance thereof and at the same time indicates the final purpose of all, we would find it in the word "kingdom"! The church has to be considered in relation to the kingdom and it has to be explained on the basis thereof. The church exists for the sake of the kingdom, preaches the message of the kingdom, lives in expectation of the full manifestation of the kingdom and should erect signposts of the kingdom in everything it does.

16. The kingdom of God is already present but will be revealed in its full glory only in the fullness of time, with the second advent of Christ.

This kingdom, which is served by the church, will not, in a futuristic sense, materialise for the first time only at the end of time, but is present even now, in our time, even though in an incomplete and provisional state and therefore often obscured.

Christ restored the revelation of the kingdom of God which had been obscured because man had fallen into sin. Therefore the church calls for obedience to God in all spheres of life.

In general terms we may say that the kingdom of God is God's sovereignty, on the one hand, and, on the other, the obedient acceptance thereof by his subjects. Wherever God reigns and obedience to Him is found, there the kingdom of God is revealed. But the fall of man into sin changed obedience into disobedience because God's sovereignty was repudiated. Christ came to re-establish this obedience so that both the reigning God and obedient man is present in His person, words and actions.

For this reason the kingdom of God is also in Jesus Christ himself. The church which preaches Christ, preaches the kingdom. In concrete terms this means a mandate to be obedient to God in all spheres of life and, in reality, this is a recognition of the fact that Christ is King of the whole of existence. And for this reason the church is concerned with the whole of human life in all its facets.

17. The true church of Christ is where the Word is truly preached, the sacraments administered and church discipline applied.

When is a church a church, and what are the conditions for a church to be a church? There are three requirements. In the first place, **the Word should be preached unadulterated.** The Bible is the source of all learning and life because it is the word that God speaks to man for all times. All that was written, was written for our edification and all that we can possibly learn of God can only be learnt in the Bible. In the Bible God approaches His people every day and in it He speaks to them, not from afar or from an Olympian height, but from their midst. For him who reads well and hears with his spiritual ear, the central things about the Bible is that it is **the voice of God.** Thus the Bible is the source and the light of the church.

Next, **there are the sacraments.** These were introduced by Christ Himself, not because of any insufficiency or lack of clarity in the Word, but for the sake of man so that he may understand and believe **better,** for the sacraments put the seal on the truths of the Word.

In the third instance, there is the **church discipline** which is designed to guarantee the purity of teaching and of life and to which members of the church voluntarily subject themselves. The discipline is designed to protect the honour of God by proscribing evil from the church, by openly condemning such evil and by preserving in this way the holy character of the congregation (Rom. 16 : 17; 1 Tim. 6 : 5). A church exists wherever these three conditions are met. In other words, believers are organised in such a way and lead such a life that in their daily lives they are living witnesses to the kingdom of God.

18. The church may be considered from various viewpoints: the triumphant and the struggling, the visible and the invisible.

On the subject of the church triumphant it is sufficient to say that it refers to the faithful who have already entered the state of heavenly beatitude. As far as the invisible church is concerned, one need say no more than that it refers to the faith of the **true** members and their expression of that faith.

The church visible is manifested as an institute and as an organism.

40

19. As institute the church is organised under the guidance of office-bearers.

The church as an institute with its assemblies, offices and preaching is an **institute** of God. The assemblies consist of the congregations of believers, the church councils, and, in the broader context, of the presbyteries and synods. The offices are those of the elders who teach and govern and of the deacons. The ministration of the church comprises the teaching of the Word and the administration of the sacraments, as well as pastoral care and charity. The administration of church discipline is part of the power to govern.

It should be noted that it is not a unique quality of the church as institution that it exists by a special grace: its unique quality is that it functions under the guidance of its officers. After all, each Christian lives in and through his faith in Christ at all times and in all spheres of life. It is moreover true that the office of all believers may also function within the church as institution. This applies in particular to auxiliary services, such as services of charity, and the catechesis, but these services should be performed under the guidance of the particular office concerned.

20. The various images used in the Bible to denote the church reveal that the church has three basic relationships: (1) to God, (2) to herself and (3) to the world.

As far as the relationship to God is concerned, it appears that the church is a unique, divine institution which must be distinguished from a society, association or even a pious community. The church is the work of the Father, the Son and the Holy Ghost. The primary foundation of the church lies in the prehistoric love of God the Father. In our time Jesus Christ is the Head of the church, while it is gathered together by the Holy Ghost. In contradistinction to humanity sinful in Adam, we have humanity reborn in Christ. This transformation was made possible by the death of Jesus Christ and man's faith in Him. Therefore faith really means an implantation in Christ – and this is equal to an implantation in His body. Christ had to redeem His body to make it His own and this body which He leads to full obedience and on behalf of which He intercedes with the Father, is the church on earth. Thus Christ is Saviour and Head, but also Advocate and Perfecter of His body, i.e. of His church on earth. Through His Word and Spirit He brings and holds His church together.

As far as her relationship to herself is concerned, it appears that the church also has an internal life or intra-ecclesiastical structure. The implantation in the body of Christ is continued in and leads to a new life in reconciliation. The faith is given a concrete form, also in the relationship with fellow believers and in this manner the communion of the saints arises. It is a life which either grows or languishes, which is built up or broken down (Ef. 4 : 12). This process of growth is either intensive or extensive, qualitative or quantitative. The body grows and is nourished when and in as far as it allows Christ, His Spirit and His Word to live within it. When people are willing to be equipped for their service for the development of the body, when they become ever more obedient to their Head, when they lay aside the old man with his works and assume the new man who is regenerated in knowledge and in the image of his Creator, Christ is revealed more and more, and His body grows when the members of His body accept and forgive one another, teach and admonish one another, and do whatever they do in word and deed, either alone or together, only in the name of the Lord Jesus and thank God through Him (Col. 3 : 1-17), the kingdom of God is revealed.

As far as its relationship with the world is concerned, i.e. with humanity in its state of sinful corruption – the church has a twofold responsibility. In the first place it must see the world as the field where God wishes to establish His kingdom and where the church therefore has to preach the message of this kingdom. The church may not withdraw into a state of self-sufficiency or self-concern and thus ignore the plight of the human race. If it should do so, it would run the risk of sacralisation, with the end result the barren structure of the sectarian figure. On the other hand, if the church should not realise that it is dealing with **sinful** man and that it should therefore not become part of the world, thereby losing its own identity and uniqueness, it will fall into profanation. The dialectic tension between the church and the world of sin is designated in the well-known words: the church is **in** the world but not **of** the world. Both these conditions – **in** and **of** – should be acted upon in earnest. The church's relationship with the world should be characterised by its involvement in and its antithesis to the world. If the church should concern itself only with its relationship to the world, the end result would be horizontalism. Then the vertical level, expressing its relationship to God, and its eschatological expectation of His Second Coming to finally and fully restore His Kingdom, would be obscured or underemphasized.

21. The church may not withdraw from the world. On the contrary, as a pentecostal church it should claim the world for God.

The church's involvement with the world will be revealed in the church's realisation that, like itself, the world, too, is the object of God's love (John. 3 : 16). Therefore it is the task of the church at all times to regard the world with love and to seek to claim it for God. Thus, the church which withdraws itself from the world into a domain entirely of its own, transforms the incarnation of Christ into a wholly spiritual concept, whereas the fact that God **truly** became man in Christ, means that the church too was truly set in the actual world as such. With Pentecost the church became church of the world, church for the world and church for all peoples. The church must show the deepest interest in everything that concerns the world. Thus the church cannot merely reject in a negative manner the cultural development of the world, but in this matter, too, the recreative grace of God will have to be brought to bear and the preaching of obedience has to be carried on at all times.

22. While it is in the world, the church must nevertheless be different to the world in order to be able to perform its function in the world.

The antithesis will be revealed in the fact that the church, **in** its openness to the world, must realise that it is the salt and the light of the world; that its members are still temporary sojourners and foreigners **in** the world. If it wishes to fulfil its task in the world, the church must guard against the danger of becoming conformed to this world (Romans 12 : 2) and keep itself undefiled **in** the world (James 1 : 27). Inasmuch as the world lives in enmity with God, all friendship with the world is unconditionally condemned (James 4 : 4; 1 John. 2 : 15). The church is therefore called upon to persuade the entire society to be obedient to the demands of God. If there is no tension between church and society, it means that either society has been reborn in Christ or the church has begun to conform to the world.

23. A people and the diversity of peoples like the church itself, serve the kingdom of God.

The relationship between church and people is one aspect of the church's relationship with the world. We have already discussed the concept **"people"** in some detail at the beginning of this report. Suffice it to say that the significance, or lack of it, of the existence of a people is not determined by any (supposed) inherent superiority, but by its conscious or unconscious collaboration in the progress of the kingdom of God. The diversity of peoples, too, must be accepted as **the will of God in His mercy** for the reality of this world, with a view to the advancement of the kingdom of God.

43

24. When the church is termed the "people of God," it does not mean that the church is a national church in the sense that Israel as a nation was "people of God", or that peoples of various nations are "people of God" in the same sense that the church is a community of God.

Holy Scripture is concerned with the revelation of the acts of God the Father through Jesus Christ and the Holy Ghost with people in order to gather and build a **new** people, the ecclesia. In a certain sense **all** peoples are indeed "people of God", for the whole earth is His (Ex. 19 : 5 and Romans 3 : 29), but the members of the church are the people of God in a very special sense of the word: in the fact that through and in their **faith** they know themselves to belong to God and openly proclaim the fact. Since **faith,** as the fruit of predestinating grace, is the decisive factor in the shaping of this new people, **church and people are not the same,** because the latter is concerned with relationships of descent and cultural ties and **not** with faith. Only if they should indeed be the same, would one be able to talk of a national church, which is never mentioned in the Bible. The concept of a national or state church is false. Instead, we uphold the Scriptural concept of a denominational, confessional church within the national context.

25. The church may not be indifferent to the people, because the raison d'être of the church is to be found in the people.

Although church and people do not coincide, the church nevertheless finds its existence amongst the people. If the church is denied this, the kingdom of God will suffer; and if the kingdom should suffer, so naturally would people and church. Spiritually the church may therefore not be indifferent to its actual existence and survival in the midst of a particular people. **For in this imperfect reality** it is the will of God that both church and people should serve the kingdom in a concrete way and that they should seek their own destiny as instruments of the kingdom.

26. In so far as the people is one of the society structures willed by God and designed to serve the advancement of the kingdom, the church must accept the people as servant of God. Therefore, the church may serve the people, but with the proviso that this service should follow the norms of the Word and that mutual boundaries should be respected.

There is an intimate relationship between church and people as regards both their existence and the fulfilment of their calling. The church preaches the message of redemption **to** the people and draws the faithful – those who become members of the church – from the people. Thus the church draws its members from the people and has to regard the people among whom it works and exists with loyalty and a readiness to serve, but at the same time it will know that all fellow-citizens are not co-religionists and that not all co-religionists are necessarily fellow-citizens. The church will have to see the nation as the area in which the preaching of the message of re-conciliation must be carried on.

Furthermore, the church offers the people spiritual guidance, for in its preaching and intercession the church concerns itself with the plight and social circumstances of the people. In the material sphere, too, the church reaches out to the people and diaconal care encompasses more than merely the fellow-believers. This sacerdotal service to the people is not rendered for general humanitarian reasons, but to witness to the fact that man is not master of his own life but that his fate has been decided, that his needs are being provided for, even though he might not yet or no longer accept the Provider.

But at all times it will have to be taken in consideration that each society has its own nature and structure and must abide by its own laws. Thus church and nation each has its own structure and is sovereign in its own sphere, despite the intimate relationship between the two. Mutual boundaries will therefore have to be respected, for as soon as the church attempts to churchify the entire national life, it becomes a totalitarian institution which abrogates the principle of sovereignty in individual spheres. No nation, not even a Christian nation, is subject to the sovereignty of the church. The nation is, however, subject to the ultimate authority and discipline of Christ and His Word.

27. The church as institution may in no circumstances take part in politics.

The fulfilment of its calling presupposes that the involvement of the church with the people will never mean complete identification with the people. The church must never allow its calling and character to be prejudiced by identifying itself with the wishes and demands of the people or by making the national objectives of the people its own. Thus the church may never become a political institution which forsakes its own spiritual calling by pronouncing for or against the power structure within the state or in favour of one or other political party. The church should be **associated** with the people but it should not become part of that people, for in the latter case it would repudiate its own being and autogenous existence.

28. The church must fulfil its prophetic, priestly and kingly function also towards the people.

Like all other spheres, a community of people is no neutral sphere. It is both the object of God's loving concern and the area where Satan manifests his power. Inasmuch as the destructive power of Satan is also revealed in the nation, the church will have to be clear and incisive in its testimony. This critical function of the church, which it must perform in respect of every other facet of society, should never become merely judicial, but must at all times retain its priestly and prophetical character. Thus the church is **for** the people and at the same time **against** the sins of the people, for the sake of the preservation of the people – in the same way as the church fights against the sins in its own bosom for the sake of its own self-preservation. The church will therefore forsake its calling unless it is clear from its ministry that it is indeed **for** the people and at the same time **against** the sins of the people (cf. the function of the prophets of the Old Testament).

29. In its visible structure the church should not exist divorced from the people to whom it must preach the Word of God. It is the calling of the church by its missionary and church life to subject the values and most profound convictions in the culture of a people to the Word of God at all times, in the expectation that the basic Christian convictions will to an ever increasing extent become the essence thereof. Therefore a diversity of peoples can lead to a diversity of indigenous churches.

It obviously follows from this concept that in the establishment and organisation of the church the people among whom the church is founded is of the utmost importance. When the church draws its members from a particular people and they are called upon to practice their Christian fellowship within the context of their church, i.e. to give expression to their obedience to Christ, it is only to be expected that the church will assume a particular cultural content to coincide with the people among whom it has been established. This unique cultural heritage should to an ever-increasing extent be brought "into obedience unto Christ" and sanctified accordingly. Just as humanity has been subdivided into various peoples and nations, the one church of God also comprises various types, differing among one another, according to the differences inherent in the people from among whom the church draws its members. The fact that there are English, Afrikaans, German, Bantu, and other churches is a phenomenon which is closely related to the diversity of peoples concerned

46

and ti must be considered principally against this background. Thus, though the church is essentially one, in this dispensation it reveals itself in a pluriform manner. It must be emphasised that this pluriformity of the church in no way implies the subordination of one formation or formations to another or others. The only legitimate connotation of the pluriformity of the church consists therein that there are co-ordinates, which develop as various, but in all respects autonomous, visible formations of the one invisible body of Christ.

30. In our dispensation the church of Christ displays a pluriformity which is directly related to the diversity of peoples, but it is not a closed community in the sense that it is meant for members of one people only.

Just as members of a certain people or nation may **in principle** not be prevented from becoming members of another people or nation, so members of one "national" church may not be forbidden to become members of another "national" church. In other words, **in principle** there is no exclusive national church in the sense that no believer from the ranks of any other people may join it if he should choose to do so, even if we should uphold the importance of national identity for the preaching of the gospel and for experiencing the communion of the saints. A separate church is certainly not a closed church.

If, however, such a transfer of membership should disturb the order and peace of both church and people (peoples or sections of the people) to such an extent that the kingdom of God is no longer served, that the fellowship of believers and their ability to serve should suffer and the nation or nations concerned should find it difficult or impossible to give full expression to their national identity – in these circumstances a temporary arrangement against the transfer of membership cannot be condemned since it would enhance the well-being of the churches concerned.

31. The preaching of the church is not designed to provide a blueprint of action for all spheres of life, but rather to proclaim relevant principles for the guidance of experts in the various fields.

The Word of God has been entrusted to the church and believers must use this Word as prophets, priests and kings of God. The church preaches the Word of God prophetically and seeks to persuade people to be obedient to God. This obedience does not comprise a detailed programme of action for all spheres of life, because for the church to devise such a programme would mean to exceed the limits of its experts as though it had all wisdom in all fields at its command. It merely proclaims the promises and commandments of God and appeals to the conscience of all people. This does not, however, imply that the receiver of the gospel message is thereby given unlimited authority in respect of the application of the gospel. The methods of application must also be critically weighed. Rather than prescribe solutions, the church would in its preaching criticise and reject unacceptable solutions. Thus there is no limitation to the **fields** or spheres in which the church may preach the Word, but there is a limitation placed on the **function** which the church may fulfil in those various fields. The church preaches God's Word for **all** spheres of life, but it remains the function of the believing specialists to decide precisely how the Word is to be obeyed in practice in their own particular fields, with this proviso that their results should again be tried to see whether they are in accordance with the Word of God.

This means that the particular ecclesiastical offices may never usurp the general function of all believers in the spheres of state and society. The minister of religion would exceed the bounds of his commission if he should, for instance, try to usurp the duty of the government by promulgating laws. He would also be guilty of overreaching if he should try to usurp the function of the philosopher by establishing a set of principles for all the areas of science. In its priestly function the church is concerned about the needs of individuals and groups of people: it bears them in mind in its intercession and relieves their distress through charitable services. As kings in the kingdom of God, the church reigns over sin through the Word, by means of admonishment and discipline. The church does all this not by trying to churchify society in its entirety, but by Christianizing it by calling upon everybody to erect recognizable tokens or sign posts of the kingdom of God in this world.

32. The unity of the church is derived from the work of the one God in respect of the church: in its origin, destiny, equipment and its source of life. There should, however, also be unity of confession, of fellowship and of service.

As far as the unity of the church is concerned, one should draw a distinction between the unity **given** and the unity **demanded**. The given unity is derived from the fact that the church is the work of one Father, one Son and one Holy Ghost (Eph. 4 : 3-6). Therefore the church has one origin, one destiny and one equipment and one life source, i.e. Holy Scripture. Correlated to this is the fact that the church has but one faith, one hope and one love to practise. Unity demanded comprises one redeemed life of which there are various aspects. Firstly, **unity of confession.** He who proclaims Christ his Saviour and Head is one with and becomes one with all other men who proclaim the same. Thus the wrestling for truth – the truth of the confession – is a concrete manifestation of the struggle for unity and, in fact, proof of unity.

There is also unity of fellowship: Those who believe and therefore share in the acts of salvation of God in Christ through the Holy Ghost will at all times have to share one another's lives. In the church of Christ there will be a common participation, not only in the blessings issued by the Lord, but also in afflictions; in suffering (Hebr. 10 : 33), in comfort (2 Cor. 1 : 7), in tribulation and in patience (Revelations 1 : 9).

The church is also called to unity in service: The church will have to serve in this world for Christ's sake; it will have to concern itself with distress on both the personal and the social level, with the personal aspects of hunger and illness, the general economic aspects of exploitation and injustice, homelessness and poverty, whether these be permanent conditions of distress which arise from sudden disasters. He who serves this way, at the same time also proves before the world something of the unity of the Christian testimony.

33. The unity of the church is not only an invisible but also a visible reality.

The unity of the church is characterised in a remarkable way in the Bible. It says: ". . . that they may be made perfect in one; **and that the world may know** that thou hast sent me . . ." (John. 17 : 23). Christ himself said that in one way or another the unity of the church will have to be observed by the world: it must be **seen, heard** and **experienced.** Therefore, it must be a unity which differs from the kind of unity which ordinarily becomes visible in the world.

This unity is thus not merely a spiritual unity residing in the invisible relationship with God or a specific attitude or feeling in the hearts of the faithful: it must also find concrete expression in word and deed. The unity of the church is not a purpose in itself and has no publicity value if it remains merely an abstract idea or secret conviction. It is inconceivable that the unity of all true children of God should not be revealed in some way, but it need not be revealed in one institution. Without doubt the church has to proceed with due care and wisdom and has to take account of the historical situation, of the incompleteness of reality as well as of the level of civilisation, the degree of maturity and the diversity of peoples. All compulsory and demonstrative manifestations of unity ought to be rejected, for

4

these may seriously disturb the established order in church and society.

34. Despite, and in the midst of, all the differences among peoples, Holy Scripture knows only one church of Christ in the world.

Holy Scripture knows no multiplicity or plurality of churches. The church is one and not more than one. In Gal. 3 : 28 Paul says: "There is neither Jew nor Greek, there is neither bond nor free, there is neither male nor female: for ye are all one in Christ Jesus". This diversity of races (Jew and Greek), status (bond and free) and sexes (male and female) have both soteriological and ecclesiological significance. Soteriological, because Paul states that the salvation of all those mentioned here is only in Jesus Christ: the Jew does not find his salvation in a way different to that of the Greek, and a man is redeemed in the same way as a woman. But it also has an ecclesiological significance, for when they have been redeemed, they are no longer individuals, strangers to one another or independent of one another, but they join one body which binds them together as a unity in Jesus Christ.

Mention is indeed made in the Bible of **churches:** the church of Galatia, of Asia, of Macedonia (1 Cor. 16 : 1, 19, 2 Cor. 8 : 1), etc. But this is merely **a diversity within the same church.** Holy Scripture does not reject this type of diversity, but it does reject the diversity which degenerates **into contradistinctions** (1 Cor. 5 : 1, et seq.).

The pluriformity of churches which is related to, and the consequence of, the diversity of peoples, may be a diversity **within the same church,** as body of Christ. But then the unity will have to be manifested in one way or another.

35. Disruption of the church arises when the unity of the church is threatened by sinful division, while pluriformity is justified by the teachings of the Bible.

The New Testament and, more particularly, the second section of the Epistle to the Ephesians, warn **against the danger of discord and division.** According to the apostle, the unity of the church is a gift of God, but at the same time a gift that should never be accepted as a matter of course. It should be assiduously sought and protected if it is not to be lost. He warns against some of the threats the church of the New Testament and of all ages has faced (Eph. 4 : 31; cf. also Philip. 4 : 2, 3 John (Diótrefes); Acts 15, where fellowship on the basis of grace, received through faith and expressed in baptism, is proclaimed as the foundation of the church, as against the legalistic demands of the Judaisers.)

The division and disunity of the church, as it is manifest on earth today, must at all times be admitted and confessed as a sin; because there is but one Lord of the church, there can be but one church, the body of Christ, his people on earth.

36. An aspect of the demanded unity of the church is the contact which the churches must maintain with one another on the basis of confession and which is expressed in the concept true ecumenicity.

While the church may not acquiesce in its divisions and must at all times confess these as sinful, **it may not, on the other hand, evade the question of truth in its search for unity.** Genuine, meaningful Christian unity can only be founded on Jesus Christ and his Word. Church unity can never be sought and found in anything but the gospel.

A mere amalgamation of churches as they exist today would be a monstrosity. Therefore, in all ecumenical contact the search should be to discern the will of God revealed in His Word. All churches should be prepared to renew themselves according to the precepts of the Word. To the degree in which this happens the unity of all believers in Christ will become more real also **on earth.** Church unity without unity as regards the basic Christian confession would be without meaning. Therefore, the demand for renewal according to God's Word should at all times be emphasised in the search for unity. This applies to all churches, but a certain measure of elasticity will always have to be applied. To make complete uniformity of conviction on every jot or tittle among all churches a prerequisite for unity would be to expect far too much. The essence of the gospel will have to serve as criterion at all times. For us, as members of the Reformed churches the attitude of Calvin is a glorious example in this respect.

37. Ecumenicity means a meeting of churches which take one another seriously in all maters in the light of the Word of God.

In practice a distinction should be drawn between the demand for an ecumenical dialogue and that for the actual unification of churches. When the deliberations are not concerned with the actual unification of churches but merely an ecumenical dialogue between churches with a view to the promotion of unity and the elimination of misconceptions and misunderstandings, they will obviously take place on the basis of matters comprising the essence of the gospel, even though every participant in the dialogue may approach the deliberations from his own comprehensive theological position. If the dialogue should proceed to the point where a decision is taken to amalgamate two or more churches, the agreement should cover all essential matters of faith.

38. Ecumenical dialogue and accommodation have their own limitations; these are contained in the boundaries of the church itself. No ecumenical association may be entered into with the "false church".

As churches, we are essentially concerned with all other churches in which something of Jesus Christ is still to be found. Only the entirely false churches would have to be eliminated completely. As far as these are concerned, we can at the most bear testimony to the truth: we can no longer conduct a dialogue as fellow Christians. But we should be prepared to conduct a dialogue with all churches which still contain something of Christ and the gospel, with the proviso that in such dialogue and deliberations we have the opportunity of bearing testimony in an unfettered way to the gospel as we understand it, and to disassociate ourselves from any decision or pronouncement to which we are unable to subscribe.

39. The sanctity of the church is derived from its implantation in Christ and thus the church is expected to sanctify life.

The second attribute of the church is its **sanctity**. The church is that group of people chosen by God Himself to be used by Him in a special manner. The sanctity of the church is derived from its separation from sin and its implantation in Christ. Thus the church belongs to an order of its own and the sanctity of the church points to its status before God. But what the church possesses **in Christ** must also be realised in itself. The condition of sanctity enjoins the church to the sanctification of all life. In concrete terms, this means a continued and deepening obedience to God's Word.

40. The universality of the church means that the church reaches into the entire world, that it preaches the whole of revealed truth and that it demands complete obedience from all people.

The third attribute of the church is **its universality**. In the sense of comprising the whole or being aligned to the whole, the universality may point to **the world as a whole.** The church is not confined to a specific people, but comprises **all** peoples of **all** times **in whatever** parts of the world they lived and still live. In this sense the church comprises extensively not only the entire inhabited area of the earth, but also extends itself along the longitude and latitude of time. Universality also points to revealed **truth in its entirety.** This means that the church is profoundly concerned with the complete truth of what God has revealed from the beginning and which has been preserved for us in the Bible. The struggle of the church for the formulation and reformulation of truth under the guidance of the Spirit, is, however, never complete. Universality is also related to the **whole field of obedience.** The message of the gospel asks from us no half-hearted acceptance, but a genuine and complete surrender of man in all spheres of life. The universality of the church may be summarised in the following sentence: **Christ all in all at all times, and at all times all in all.**

41. The sovereignty of Christ on earth is visibly revealed in the church – incomplete and provisional, it is true, but nevertheless driving forward to the fullness at the end of time.

The attributes of the church lead us to conclude that the church is that part of humanity which Christ has claimed for Himself so that His merciful sovereignty may be revealed in prophetic provisionality in the lives of people – prophetically provisional, because the church is not static but a dynamic quantity on the way from sin to the fullness of God's sovereignty; the **people** of the Lord in His restless searching for the peoples of the world; the **sign,** ever increasing in clarity and fullness, of the kingdom of the triune God, already present but ever coming.

HORIZONTALISM AND THE HORIZONTAL DIMENSION OF THE CHURCH'S WORK.

42. Viewpoint of horizontalism.

42.1 Horizontalism does not appear in a systematically developed form, but is a general tendency, particularly in ecumenical thinking.

Horizontalism is a term widely used at the moment to indicate a specific conception of the calling of the church in the world – mostly in a disapproving manner or as an admonishment.
This conception has been current in the ecumenical movement for a long time, but during the past decade in particular it has gained so much ground that it is now governing in ever increasing measure the action programmes and official actions of the World Council of Churches.

To express this concept in a few sentences is not an easy matter. And this is so because horizontalism is nowhere available as a systematically developed premise. Rather it is a general tendency in ecumenical discussions and pronouncements and is to be observed and evaluated in the priority which it bestows on certain matters.

42.2 Horizontalism is the emphasising of the significance of God's redemptive work for life on earth, at the expense of the significance of redemption itself.

Horizontalism is the opposite pole of what may be regarded as a pietist vision of the revelation of God's salvation. In contrast to the conception of the Christian religion as an inner cult of piety, horizontalism emphasises service to the world. Instead of relating grace mainly to the narrow objective of the absolution of guilt (i.e. the personal relationship between God an the sinner, the salvation of the soul, and the acquisition of eternal life in the hereafter, the longing for heaven), the whole emphasis is placed on social relevance and therefore on the significance of God's redemptive work for **this** life and **this** world. Instead of regarding salvation as a spiritual concept, an answer to the spiritual anguish of man, horizontalism sees the regeneration promised in the gospel primarily as an answer to the social, economic and political needs of man, i.e. to poverty and social and political injustices whereby man is enslaved and deprived of his liberty and therefore prevented from bringing to full fruition his human qualities, according to God's wishes.

42.3 In the horizontalistic approach the church is absorbed by its relationship to the world, to the exclusion of the other relationships in which the church also finds itself.

Horizontalism is opposed to the kind of religious practice which would make of the church an introvert corporation for salvation completely isolated from the world and vertically bound up only in God and eternity. The church does not exist for its own sake, but exclusively on behalf of the world, namely as bridgehead by means of which the regenerating powers of God's kingdom can penetrate and change the world. God wishes to renew the **world** because He **loves** it. If the church wishes to be in step with God's dispensation of salvation, it will have to accept responsibility for the world, in solidarity with the distress of the world.

In terms of the foregoing, the function of the church is seen as that of giving concrete shape to God's redemptive act of salvation by devoting itself to the establishment of a **responsible society** in which peace, justice and freedom will be guaranteed to every man. In order to execute this commission, the church cannot concentrate its service to the world merely in succour and welfare work on an incidental and sporadic basis. In order to promote the establishment of a responsible society, the church has to undertake a comprehensive programme of action with a view to identifying and combating the **sources** of the various forms of social, economic and political distress. And these sources are not to be found so much in the sin and vices of individual people as in the corruption of the traditional supra-individual community **structures** in which injustice and suppressions have been institutionalised. If the church wishes to carry out its function in the world, it will have to devote itself to the radical transformation of the world community by word and deed.

43. Evaluation of horizontalism.

43.1 In terms of horizontalism the church is not only called upon to make a thorough study of social problems but also to be directly involved with these.

In order to carry out this commission, the church first has to make an intensive study of social, economic and political problems. In the light of knowledge thus acquired, the church also has to participate actively in the shaping of social and political opinion, to exert continuous and calculated pressure on the authorities and policy makers in the various sectors of society and at the same time give its active and financial support to social and political reform and liberation movements which seek to bring about a change in the basic structure of society.

43.2 An evaluation of horizontalism should be preceded by an admission that the church does indeed have a function at the horizontal level.

To adopt a negative attitude towards the emphasis which horizontalism places in religious practice **a priori,** would not be in accordance with the Reformed tradition in which the horizontal responsibility and calling of the church in respect of the world and society have always been acknowledged and honoured. The Reformed churches and theology have at all times in true piety and devotion sought to serve the kingdom of God in all spheres of life. In addition to that, salvation has always been interpreted as being related not only to eternal life in the hereafter, but also to the needs of man in the world of today – and on a sound Biblical basis.

Thus, when Christians today demand that special attention be given to the urgent problems of their society, their efforts should not **a priori** be regarded with suspicion. The important question is, however, **in what form** and **with what expectations** the attention is given.

43.3 The Bible does not admit of the false contradistinction between vertical and horizontal.

Rejecting a one-sided, verticalistic and individualistically-orientated notion of salvation is not necessarily horizontalism in the meaning described above. The Bible rejects such a dilemma between verticalism and horizontalism. In the case of the prophets of the Old Testament it is precisely the knowledge of the Lord and the rejoicing in His communion which inspires an intense concern for the anguish and pain caused by social injustice and malpractices.

According to the summary of the law, the final passage of Matthew 25 and the first letter to John, love of and service to God do not exclude love and concern for one's neighbour: on the contrary, it is specifically and fully included.

43.4 The Bible gives priority to the vertical relationship between God and man and bases therein man's horizontal relationship to the world.

At the same time it is clear that the Bible gives priority to man's personal relationship with and his love for God. Therein lies the only consolation in life and death. To bear testimony to this is the first and foremost calling of the church in the world: "For God so loved the world, that he gave his only Son, that **whoever** believes on him should not perish, but have eternal life" (John. 3 : 16 R.S.V.). When the calling to render succour to one's neighbour and the church's responsibility for human relations are emphasised so heavily that this basic message is swept under the table, the fundamental message of the gospel is adulterated and the horizontal calling itself loses its Christian motivation and quality and is no longer to be distinguished from secular and humanistic actions. That love of and care for one's neighbour is so closely linked in the Bible with love for God, serves, on the one hand, as a warning against a one-sided preoccupation with the vertical dimension of salvation. On the other hand, the fact that God's acts of salvation are primarily directed at personal redemption may not be abused as an alibi for a reluctance or unwillingness to acknowledge and accept the social implications of salvation.

43.5 Only he who lives in the new life granted him through the resurrection of Jesus Christ is capable of regenerative work in this world.

The breakthrough of God's regenerative grace in this world through the resurrection of Jesus Christ may not be divorced from the cross by which we have come to know the judgment of God on this passing aeon of sin and death. The lifeblood of the church is its faith in God's victory over this world, and hence also the expectation of a new world which will not be the achievement of man but altogether the handiwork of God only.

The expectation of God's world does not, of course, imply quietism on the part of the Christian church. The horizontalist school of thought would be right in condemning such an attitude. The indicative on which and by which faith exists, comprises also an imperative. In the gospel the law is the essential guide-line for the new life which God has given in His mercy. Faith without good works is moribund, if not dead. Both church and Christians are called upon by acts of love to erect signposts of the new world to which God is leading us. Thus Paul may even use the expression "God's fellow-workers" (1 Cor. 3 : 9).

The context in which this expression is used (1 Cor. 3 : 4-8), casts a special light on the work and activities of believers. It is God who decides whether the seed of renewal sown by human testimony and activities will germinate, grow and bear fruit. This perspective on faith guards the "fellow-worker" against a high-handed activism, in competition with the work of God, in which attempts are made to bring about the regeneration quite independently of God. The horizontalist school of thought is certainly guilty of such high-handed activism which strives in impatience and haste to bring about the new world which God has promised. For it tends to regard the salvation of the world too much as the happy result of human endeavour. A gospel without law and faith without works undoubtedly lead to introversion and a paralysis of the church's service to and in the world. But law without the gospel, works without faith and haste without expectations lead to an equally impermissible legalistic approach and a secularisation of salvation.

If the defeat of the forces of sin and corruption is sought only in the transformation of society, we are dealing with an aberration which does not give due acknowledgement to either the cross or the resurrection of Christ, in their proper relationship to one another. For it is the message of the cross which prevents us from underestimating the forces of darkness and hence preserves us from the misconception that God's promises of salvation can be fulfilled by human endeavour within the horizon of the here and now. The resurrection of Christ is the basis of the Christian's expectation of a magnificent future which God Himself will bring about, in which all needs will be fulfilled and all yearnings of the entire creation stilled.

It is true that this expectation does not render the church passive: on the contrary, it inspires it to witness to this expectation and to service in the world. But a church that lives by the cross and the resurrection of Jesus Christ, cannot identify the promised salvation for the world and the coming of the kingdom of God exclusively with structural changes in society. Nor can it identify God's justice with economic and social reorganisation, or the freedom of the children of God with the democratisation of political systems.

43.6 A functionalist view of the church, in which the significance of the church is defined in terms of its service to the world, is not Biblical. The church has a liturgical dimension.

The church is the bride (i.e. the beloved!) of Christ, the body of which He is the Head. As such it has a distinctive and independent significance within the context of the coming of the kingdom of God. The church is the sphere where salvation may be joyously celebrated, where God desires to be praised and glorified. The church has a liturgical dimension.

There is no doubting the fact that God loves the world, but the way in which His world-regenerating love reveals itself is the gathering of a congregation of reconciled and redeemed sinners who as a people of chosen servants, have been called to be the salt of the earth and the light of the world.

It is not by functionalizing the church into an organisation for social reform or into a political pressure group, but rather by reliving the reconciliation and solidarity **with God** that genuine solidarity with and service to the world is guaranteed.

The church remains at all times a mission church, but particularly so because of its separate and quite different existence in the world, the different manner in which it reacts to the forces of this world through the power of the Holy Spirit – the forces of wealth, fashion, leisure, sex, money, fear for the future and such like. If this difference is there, it is in itself the greatest service which the church can render the world. If it should not be there, the entire involvement of the church with the problems of society and all its actions with a view to change would become empty activism.

THE THEOLOGY OF REVOLUTION

44. The premise of the theology of revolution.

44.1 Against the background of the horizontalist school of thought, the origin of the theology of revolution can be seen as a revolt against the status quo. This revolt is not seen primarily as one involving the use of violence, but some representatives of this theology do not exclude such use of violence.

The theology of revolution has grown from a certain dissatisfaction with the action programme associated with the concept of a "responsible society". This programme envisaged "minor steps" which would eventually lead to a fundamental democratisation of society. (Shaull, Richard: **Encounter with Revolution,** New York, 1955.) According to Shaull c.s. such a plan does not take into account the complex technical and economic structure which, as a total, integrated system dominates the modern industrialised society. It is a system in which man is materially satisfied to such an extent that he is robbed of the need, inclination and spiritual power for renewal (Marcuse, H.: **One Dimensional Man – Studies in the ideology of advanced industrial societies,** Boston, 1964.) Those who start working for change in one sector of society, are up against a total system which prevents a fundamental transformation of society. Thus a new strategy is required. Renewal can only be achieved through permanent revolutionary action, based on guerrilla tactics. People in key positions and vital institutions must at all times be pressurised by means of "teach-ins", "sit-ins" and, if need be, violence, so that in this manner they may be compelled to change the structure of the society concerned. According to Shaull, only the effective shock of limited revolutionary actions has the capacity to keep society and its institutions open and flexible and therefore susceptible to renewal and transformation.

One should, however, immediately add that, despite its radical name, this theology **does not seek to achieve its aims by violence.** Adherents of this theology often emphasise that they were not baptised "on the sword" but "on the cross".

44.2 The theology of revolution reproaches the church and its theology that it proclaims a "theology and practice of contra-revolution", i.e. a defence at all costs of the status quo and resistance to every attempt at a renewal of society. Another reproach is that the church sees the Christian expectation only as consolation with a view to a better "jenseits" and an acquiescence in "this vale of tears".

The church must go out into the world to confront it with God and the consequences of the kingdom of God. If the church does not do this, the world will enter the church.

The church is too often inclined to forget that **the cross of Jesus** did not stand in the privatissimum of the individual and personal terrain, nor in the sanctissimum of the purely religious. It stood **outside,** in the world, as the letter to the Hebrews emphasises (Metz, J. B.: **Zur Theologie der Welt,** Mainz, 1968.)

44.3 This theology reproaches the church that it pietistically narrows and superficialises sin and is unable to realise that sin is also to be found in the structures of society.

The prophets not only preached against sin on a personal basis, but particularly on the subject of **the sins of Nineveh and Asser and Babel and Edom and Samaria,** as well as those of the structure of society. For many centuries it has been the custom of church and theology to withdraw into a ghetto-type existence, to live and think only vertically, without realising that the church also has a horizontal calling. Hence society has been abandoned to man and to the devil. Because the church had pietistically narrowed the concept of sin, the humanists were often better able than Christians to notice structural sins in feudalism, slavery, colonisation and imperialism. In fact, Christians too often glossed over them or even defended them.

44.4 This theology emphasises man's responsibility in the transformation of this world.

Blumhardt's two concepts "warten und eilen" (Christof Blumhardt, born 1842, was the first to refer to these concepts, but see Karl Barth: **Klärung und Wirkung,** Berlin, 1966, p. 289) are also used as premise for the vision of the future – Peter 3 : 12: **"Looking for and hasting** unto the coming of the day of God. . ." "We do not identify the ecumenical movement with the new Jerusalem – we await. We do not identify the United Nations with the new earth – we await. We do not identify the results of social and economic improvements and political gains with the new world in which justice dwells – we await. He who waits, is not a victim of illusionism; nor does he become cynical or defeatist. He who waits, knows that the last word does not belong to hate and injustice or mistrust or inhumanity, but to justice, because the last word belongs to Him in whom we hope. Complete redemption is not yet at hand. But the Redeemer lives and is coming. But he who only waits and does not hasten, has his hands folded in his lap and use faith as a couch on which to laze. On the other hand, it is also true that he who hastens without waiting, is feverishly active without ever knowing peace and the assurance that Jesus Christ will fulfil his promises. Make haste and await, await and make haste".

44.5 The theology of revolution claims that circumstances may arise in which violent resistance or revolt could be justified, but Christians should then take care that the revolution does not degenerate into an "all-consuming Moloch".

The protagonists of this religion emphasise that even Calvin did not hesitate to profess that it was legitimate to utilise, as a last resort, resistance measures under the auspices of the lesser legal authorities. But it should be understood, as Calvin did, that recourse to rebellion could be taken only as an **ultima ratio.** Another premise is that a revolution is unlawful, immoral and unjustified unless it is inspired by a genuine love for God and one's neighbour. In such a situation the Christian's task is more difficult than ever. It is his task to caution against sadism and revolutionary romanticism. It is also his task to demythologise the revolution and to guard against the revolution degenerating into an "all-consuming" Moloch.

45. Evaluating the theology of revolution

45.1 The concept "theology of revolution" is unacceptable as a representation of the verities of the Bible. If a revolution is considered justifiable only as an ultima ratio, why does this theology bear this name? The concept of revolution is foreign to the Bible: nowhere in scripture is such a cause pleaded.

Moreover, there is always the question whether a violent revolution can ever be **anything but a Moloch** devouring its own children. In this connection one could draw attention to the powerful arguments of Hannah Arendt in her penetrating book **On Violence,** Harcourt, 1970. She demonstrates that most violent revolutions were morally unjustifiable. Surely, in most cases a revolution merely means the substitution of one group of scoundrels for another. Idle talk about revolutions and "a few more Vietnams" has become so commonplace that Charles West coined the phrase **"guerrilla theology"** (West, C.: **Technologists and Revolutionaries,** New York, 1967). Tragically the protagonists of violent revolutions apparently forget that chaos is the greatest foe of the poor and the suppressed whom the revolutionaries profess to help.

In addition, there is the question of **the norms** of the revolution. Cox states (Cox, H.: **God's Revolution and Man's Responsibility,** London, 1964 and Cox, H.: **On not leaving it to the Snake,** London, 1968) that no theology or morality can go unchallenged. If this is so, then the same must apply to all revolutions! And it certainly is strange that one never finds such a challenge in this theology. Apparently any revolution is a little better than any theology. There is, in addition, also the very real **danger of horizontalism** lurking behind every corner in this theology. Granted that the commandment of love has two poles, the first pole is still love for and obedience to God.

45.2 On the other hand, the church is convinced that a church whose thinking is reformatory, will also act in a reformatory fashion with regard to the renewal of society. We are aware that Calvin not only said "ecclesia semper reformanda", but also "societas semper reformanda", and we agree with him in this.

The church must go out in the world to confront the world with God and the demands of God's kingdom.

Sin is not merely an individual and personal state of being but is transferred by man to his deeds and actions and also to his various enterprises in society. Hence the prophets proclaimed the judgment of God not only on individuals but also on cities, peoples and whole regions of the world.

The responsibility of man is not confined to the deed, as the theology of revolution is wont to teach: it must also have room for expectations.

The theology of revolution runs the risk of degenerating into a functionalist view of the church, in which the church becomes a mere organisation (among others) for social reform or a political pressure group. The church also has a liturgical dimension. According to the Bible the church is the place where salvation is joyously celebrated and God is praised.

Obviously, the worship of God in church must also lead to service of God in everyday life, for the work of Christ, when accomplished, is not only directed at the transformation of man, but also to that of society, indeed to the renewal of the whole earth. The church must fulfil its calling by moving between the Scylla of political intrigue, on the one hand, and the Charybdis of dereliction of duty, on the other. A gospel-without-law and faith-without-the-gospel, works-without-faith, and haste-without-expectations, on the other hand, lead to an equally impermissible legalistic approach and a secularisation of salvation.

Chapter 3

The Church and Social Justice

46. The fundamental position.

46.1 Basic Biblical concepts.

The message of Holy Scripture must remain the fundamental basis for the determination of relationships between people. Because man is created in the image of God, the basic concepts and norms for his life are love, justice, truth and peace. These arise from his reconciliation with God in Christ, by regeneration and renewal (2 Cor. 5 : 17). On this basis the faithful are called upon to erect signposts of the kingdom of God even in this dispensation, including the sphere of social relations.

46.2 The task of the church.

It is the primary task of the church to preach the Word of God and to equip its adherents for service in all spheres of life, which includes their own society. Thus, the Christian must be the salt of the earth and the light of the world in all spheres of life. This means that in its preaching the church must also call upon its adherents to apply the principles of the kingdom of God in the social and political sphere. (Acts of the Synod of the Ned. Geref. Kerk in S.A., Report 5a, especially page 18; Die N.G. Kerke in S.A. en Rasseverhoudinge, p. 18 h (iii) 20, 33 and RES, Acts 1963 and Acts 1968, Majority Report D6).

46.3 The church's message of reconciliation.

The church must preach the kingdom's prophetic message of reconciliation and healing. At the same time it must denounce sin and seek to correct sinful structures in society. In executing this function the church should not merely be concerned with the promotion of popular opinions, nor should it seek to hide behind opinions which cannot be justified according to Scripture. In fact, wherever the Word of God should demand it, the church should fulfil its prophetic function in spite of popular opinion.

46.4 Neighbourly love according to the Bible.

The Scriptural commandment of neighbourly love is the decisive norm for social justice. This commandment should always be realised in practice in all political, economic and social situations. The social justice of the New Testament therefore also comprises such practical matters as fair wages, decent employment conditions and faithful service on the part of the employee.

46.5 Social injustice.

Social injustice should be seen as a consequence of the sinful nature of man and its pervading influence in man's social structures. The church must take into account the fact that it works and lives in a reality imperfected by sin, but it may not acquiesce in this situation: it must do everything in its power within its own sphere to realise the message of redemption of Christ and his kingdom amidst "a crooked and perverse" generation (Phil. 2 : 15).

47. The church and relationships between peoples.

47.1 The church and the particular population relationships in Southern Africa.

In Southern Africa the church is called upon to be the light and salt in a complicated set of population relationships: several highly disparate peoples which differ substantially from one another, i.a. in level of civilisation, have to live together in one country.

The inequality among these peoples, particularly as a result of such factors as history and development, places a heavy burden of responsibility on the privileged peoples and societies to let justice be done to all, particularly because certain measures, essential to maintain order in certain situations, may cause suffering and hardship for some. The church is specially called to be the "conscience" of the community and at all times to place such measures in proper perspective in the light of Scripture.

In this imperfect world of ours there is, on the one hand, the temptation of egoism, exploitation and discrimination by the privileged against the less privileged group and, on the other hand, the temptation for the latter group not to accept responsibility for their own development. Both these temptations are manifested in human relationships.

47.2 The church and the factual, practical situation.

In its teaching of social justice and Christian relationships in Southern Africa, the church must at all times take into account the actual, practical situation, without accepting this situation as normative.

In considering its position in respect of the various disparate peoples inhabiting the same country, the church should take cognisance of both the unity and the diversity of the human race.

The unity entails a common cultural heritage which acts as a bridge among the various peoples. The diversity bestows on each people its own culture which is its unique possession. Although various processes are in operation which are increasing the common cultural heritage and drawing the peoples closer together, the church should not fulfil its calling in such a way that the unique cultural possessions of the various peoples are destroyed, but that both the leaders of the various peoples and the peoples themselves will seek to preserve and develop what is their own and, at the same time, be just in their mutual relationships, according to the commandment of neighbourly love.

The processes which increase the common cultural heritage are, inter alia, industrialisation, the increase in the volume of Western material goods and the means of communication. The development of educational facilities and the preaching of the Word of God by the church, reaching right across the boundaries between peoples, are also equalising processes of substantial import.

In its call to repentance and sanctification the church wishes to establish a new philosophy of life and of the world which will transcend the boundaries among peoples and forge strong bonds among them.

As an example of the changing situation, we can refer to the master-servant relationship which until a few decades ago was accepted as a reasonable and justifiable basis for Black-White relationships, but which now no longer exists in the same way.

Stereotyped images derived from obsolete situations often still determine the behaviour of people and lead to embarrassment and friction, especially in their contact with the emerging ranks of higher status among the developing peoples. New concepts and conduct are required in the new situation.

In spite of the fact that there is an increase in the common cultural heritage of peoples who live in the same country, the facts of the situation indicate that these common cultural possessions are largely material. The deeper, intrinsic cultural possessions – those concerned with a philosophy of life, and world view, norms and values – are highly conservative in nature and show only minor changes in the course of a few generations.

Although there are many superficial similarities between peoples and cultural possessions common to all, the intrinsic cultural possessions serve to emphasise the identity of each people. It is precisely this fact that renders the acknowledgement of the diversity of peoples so important. This is a sine qua non for any responsible, realistic and practical policy by which relations among various disparate peoples in the same country must be regulated with the objective of preserving peace and equitable order in the best possible way.

47.3 The church and inter-people relations:

The church believes that a sound mutual understanding is essential for the establishment of good relationships among peoples, particularly those living within the borders of the same country. This should be coupled with the acknowledgement of the diversity of peoples which grants each a full opportunity to preserve and develop its own identity.

A more relaxed, spontaneous and natural relationship among the various disparate population groups of South Africa is essential. Despite encouraging efforts to establish better relations, there are signs of estrangement, misunderstanding, prejudice and tension among the various population groups. It is not easy to acquire a sound mutual understanding if contact between members of the various population groups is reduced to a minimum.

Sound population relationships demand mutual understanding and appreciation. Natural and spontaneous contact between members of the various population groups does not necessarily imply the obliteration of the identity of the groups concerned. On the contrary, it may lead to a better understanding and appreciation of the various national identities. For this reason communication and mutual understanding should be promoted by open dialogue, consultations and joint planning in all relevant spheres of human endeavour.

48. The church and socio-economic development.

48.1 The involvement of the church.

The church cannot stand aloof from the socio-economic problems of less developed people or of developing regions and peoples. The gospel is concerned with the man as a whole, with his spiritual as well as his material needs.

The RES of Lunteren, 1968, declares in its recommendations on race relations: "Christians in general and the church in particular bear a responsibility towards members of all races who suffer from poverty, underdevelopment and political oppression. Believers should be willing to bend every effort to alleviate the suffering of such peoples" (**Acts and Reports of Reformed Ecumenical Synod,** Lunteren 1968, Study Report: Race Relations, Recommendations no. 8). See also **Verslag van die Ad Hoc-kommissie van die Raad van Kerke,**

1956, Beginselverklaring, par. 7 in **Die N.G. Kerke in Suid-Afrika en Rasseverhoudinge**, p. 17.

The Bible describes the riches of the earth as gifts of God to man (Ps. 65 : 10 et seq.; 72 : 16; 104). God gives rain to the just and the unjust (Matthew 5 : 45).

The commandment to cultivate the earth (Gen. 2 : 15) also comprises control and development of nature by science and technology.

Man is merely the steward of the property of God (1 Peter 4 : 10) and it is his duty to administer it with responsibility and justice. In this Christ himself was an example to his church: at all times He showed great concern for the temporary plight of people and sought to alleviate it.

48.2 The concept "development".

Development is a broad concept which comprises economic-technical, socio-political and cultural development, as well as the development of man towards the realisation of the full potential with which God endows him.

Originally the emphasis was almost exclusively on economic aspects: it was seen as the duty of Western "developed" nations to grant aid to the underdeveloped countries of Africa, Asia and Latin America. Recently, however, the emphasis shifted to human development, and development came to be seen as the process of liberation and conciliation which enables people to realise their full human potential, as God intends them to do.

48.3 The share of the church.

Comprehensive development programmes for an entire area or country are the responsibility of the goverment authorities, not of the church which does not have the means, equipment or specialised knowledge for such an undertaking. The church is specially equipped with the instruments of grace, the Word and the sacraments, as well as the service of the diaconate. The material aid given by the diaconate in development and in relieving distress, albeit on a limited scale, is an indication of the breakthrough of the kingdom of God in this world.

This position is in sharp contrast to the decision by the World Council of Churches to establish, in addition to sections for missionary work and the diaconate, a section for development aid with its own development fund. In this manner the function of the church is broadened to such an extent that it is moving ever futher away from the cross of Christ as the fulcrum of its existence. In the process of consistent horizontalisation, the church runs the risk of substituting the improvement of the world instead of the preaching of the Word of God.

48.4 Spiritual and material development.

The coming of the kingdom of God may not be identified with economic development. Development aid cannot be substituted for missionary work, preaching the gospel, regeneration or conversion. For believers, God's kingdom is in the first instance a spiritual home and an invisible hope. This is not to deny that in the course of history the kingdom has manifested itself as a visible reality and that in the eye of the believer there are many manifestations of its presence. It is the calling of the church to assist in the realisation of the principles of the kingdom in this world, but the Bible sets a guideline for priorities, "But seek ye first the kingdom of God, and his righteousness; and all these things (food, clothes, material progress) shall be added unto you" (Matthew 6 : 33). In Biblical terms, therefore, development is in the first instance a spiritual concept.

All Scriptural data make it clear that in Biblical teachings on growth and development, the accent falls heavily on the spiritual aspect.

The one-sided emphasis on the material development of regions holds grave disadvantages in that it may lead to spiritual decline. Young churches may find that the industrialisation and economic development of their countries spawn a spirit of materialism, and increasing dechristianisation and secularism.

48.5 The function of the church in development.

The church must therefore consider as its prime function the creation of a spiritual basis for the development of a Christian philosophy of life and worldview, an understanding of the significance of history, the value and dignity of labour and a sense of motivation to achieve a specific purpose – i.e. participation in the coming of the kingdom of God in this world.

The church should welcome and encourage orderly and sound development instigated by the authorities and other non-church bodies. It is the function of the church to bring to the attention of the relevant authorities any plight, need or injustice that may occur.

The church itself may never ignore the plight and needs of people, but should provide assistance through a purposeful diaconate and broadly based charitable services and should activate the congregation to undertake relief services for the benefit of their neighbours.

49. Political aspects.

Our study of the data contained in the Bible has led us to the following conclusion with regard to state and church as separate institutions and instruments of God, each with its own authority, structure and functions, and the relationship between them.

49.1 Task of the church.

In the first instance, it is the function of the church to preach to its adherents the gospel of personal salvation in Christ in order to strengthen them in holy faith and to prepare them for their service in the broad sphere of the church as organism (Eph. 4 : 11-16). This aspect of the church's function is of the utmost importance, because through the life and testimony of its spiritually equipped members the church fulfils its calling to be the salt of the earth and the light of the world, to see that justice is done in all spheres of life (Col. 4 : 1), to carry the norm of God's Word into all spheres of human endeavour, including that of the central authorities charged with the complex and demanding function of governing a multinational and multiracial society.

The church also has an external function – to preach the Word of God in all spheres of life and, consequently, also to the authorities. This aspect of the church's task is not set out in so many words in the New Testament, but it is part and parcel of the essential being of the church, i.e. as aspect and instrument of the kingdom of God, on the basis of which it is called upon to preach the supremacy of Christ in all spheres of life, including that of the state.

In a multinational situation the calling of the church vis-à-vis the state is twofold:

it must preach the norms of God's Word for the mutual relationships of various groups of people and for the duties of the authorities in this situation, *and*

it must warn when injustice is being done in the implementation of national policy and the application of laws.

The church must be both bold and cautious in the fulfilment of these functions. The manner in which the church addresses itself to the central authorities is determined by the following considerations:

recognition of the fact that the authorities are an institution of God and have competency in their own sphere (Rom. 13 : 1-7). The actions of the church vis-à-vis the authorities are therefore circumscribed by the fact that the church shall honour and acknowledge the different character and competency of the authorities;

acknowledgement of the believer's function in the sphere of the state;

the fact that it is not part of the church's calling to dictate to the authorities for instance, exactly how they should regulate the intercourse and relationships between the various groups in a multinational or multiracial situation, precisely because the Bible does not provide a clear indication on the nature of the structures by which the mutual relationships should be regulated;

the nature of the church's contact with the authorities which should preferably be established and maintained through the various official church bodies;

acknowledgement that in its dealings with the authorities the church should be sure of two things: the accuracy and the expertise of its facts; and that, in each case, it is indeed giving expression to the demands of the Word of God.

The church not only has a preaching, but also an intercessionary function, with a view to the coming of the kingdom of God (according to 1 Tim. 2 : 1-4).

49.2 Function of the state.

It is the duty of the state to preserve public order within its own particular area of jurisdiction, to reconcile and regulate the legal interests of the various groups for the sake of public order, to combat evil and to preserve justice. For without this, an orderly society is not possible (cf. 1 Tim. 2 : 2-4). In all this the state should act in accordance with Biblical norms, i.e. love of God and neighbour as guide-line for the public administration of justice (cf. 2 Chron. 19 : 6). The state may use institutions of power and even the sword to keep in check the pervasive influence of sin (Rom. 13 : 4). While this system of authority is essential for the regulation of various aspects of everyday life, it may never degenerate into a totalitarian system in which the state usurps the sovereignty of other institutions in their own particular fields in order to regulate all aspects of human existence. The golden rule of sovereignty for each institution in its own sphere, of justice and of love, should be sufficient to preserve the state from revolutionary chaos and political absolutism and tyranny.

49.3 Limited responsibility of the state.

Because the state alone does not regulate the internal activities of all institutions of society, it cannot be held solely responsible for all abuses resulting from a given political system.

Industry is a separate sphere of human endeavour in our modern society. The manner in which it organises and utilises its labour and capital should also be tested by the norms of the Bible and should, in terms thereof, be called to account for its Christian bias so that it may realise the norms of justice within its own sphere.

70

49.4 Conduct of church vis-à-vis state.

As institution the church submits itself to the authority and law of the state, as far as its participation in the normal processes of justice and the exercising of its civil rights are concerned, provided the legal order does not conflict with the Word of God (Church order 65.2). It is the duty of the church to preach the Word of God to the authorities, in particular the norms of the Bible in respect of mutual relationships and social justice, and the duties of the authorities in this connection.

49.5 Human rights.

We cannot accept, purely according to the teaching of the Bible, that man has rights in the sense of claims on the basis of his own merits, as the term is generally understood today. Human rights are those rights which God has bestowed upon man as the bearer of his image so that he may be able to fulfil his duties and calling as a human being. In order to be able to fulfil his calling as a human being, man has a right to life and the propagation thereof through marriage and the creation of communities and associations, to property and to freedom of religious practice and of conscience. It is self-evident that the exercise of these rights can never be divorced from the community in which the individual lives his life. For, as an association of people, the community has collective rights on the basis of which it must fulfil its divine calling.

When it comes to the acknowledgement of rights, privileges must at all times be accompanied by responsibility. Rights and privileges may not be withheld when the claim is just.

49.6 Autogenous separate development.

A political system based on the autogenous or separate development of various population groups can be justified from the Bible, but the commandment to love one's neighbour must at all times be the ethical norm towards establishing sound inter-people relations.

49.7 The Christian and politics.

Since the Christian must apply the principles of the kingdom of God in the sphere of politics as well, he must enjoy the freedom of political thought and action, exercised in a responsible manner under the guidance of the Word and Spirit of God.

The message of reconciliation of the Bible implies that there should at all times be channels for effective communication and consultation in a multinational situation.

The Christian must at all times seek to ensure that his political thinking and actions are based on justice and righteousness.

50. Education.

50.1 The purpose of education.

Education, in the Christian sense of the word, means the preparation and equipping of man for his true purpose, i.e. service to God and to his kingdom in all spheres of life.

50.2 The role of the church in education.

In South Africa the church has always campaigned for the establishment and development of educational facilities, and in many instances it actually took the initiative in the development of new projects. At present, either directly or indirectly, the church has a hand in a large variety of educational projects covering a wide spectrum of activity.

50.3 Current position of education.

Mention should be made here, with due recognition of the achievement of the state, of the substantial progress that has been made in the provision of educational facilities for all population groups. Compared with the White, the other population groups still have a large leeway to make up and it is the duty of the church and state to assist them in doing so.

51. The church and its diaconate.

51.1 Role of the organised diaconate.

The organised diaconate of the church must seriously consider its role in relieving distress in the homelands, cities and towns and on farms.
Diaconates of the mother church must get in touch with those of the daughter churches so that the former may keep abreast of needs and relief measures may be properly channelled.

51.2 The church as voice of warning for the people.

The church must serve as the voice of warning to the nation and draw attention to poverty, low wages, poor housing and other socio-economic problems which may arise among all population groups.
There is a distinct danger that Christians may become accustomed to seeing poverty and suffering around them. Thus the church must do more to teach its members to lead a life of moderation and sobriety,

avoiding all unnecessary luxuries so that they may be better able to provide assistance to the less privileged members of society. In view of these functions, the diaconate of the church must be transformed so that it may accept the task of stimulating and activating the congregation to serve the community.

52. Bantu homelands.

52.1 The task of the church.

The church must at all times show an interest in the Bantu homelands as underdeveloped areas. It should make a continuous study of socio-economic aspects of the development of the homelands and of problems that may arise. It should at all times bring to the attention of the authorities and all other relevant bodies the needs and distress that may exist in the homelands.

The Synod appeals to all its more privileged members to participate in the economic and industrial development of the Bantu homelands through, inter alia, the programme of industrial decentralisation.

52.2 Development of the homelands.

The church welcomes all efforts on the part of the authorities and other bodies to promote the viability of the Bantu homelands. The church is convinced that the rapid economic and industrial development of the Bantu homelands should be given top priority so that these regions may become happy homes to the largest possible proportion of the various Bantu peoples. The church should promote in its members the spirit of sacrifice which is required for this project.

52.3 Tenure and division of land.

Within the framework of autogenous (separate) development sufficient viable living space (Lebensraum) for the various population groups is of the utmost importance; hence the state should continue to devote its attention to the fair and just handling of this problem.

53. Bantu in White areas.

The Synod has taken note of the position of Bantu in White areas, of many problems which still exist, and also of the substantial progress made during the past few years in the provision of housing, recreational facilities and social services.

The Synod has with appreciation taken note of the continued work of its commission for liaison with the authorities, which is in constant contact with the Department of Bantu Administration and

Development for deliberations on problems which may exist or arise for the church in this multinational country.

The Synod also took cognisance of the fact that the church has given development aid through its various commissions. Since the last Synod, matters such as the following have been discussed with the authorities:

Resettlement schemes and conditions in the townships;

Wage structures and pensions;

Migrant labour and everything associated with it;

Development of border industries;

Transport facilities between city and residential area.

The Synod once again confirmed that it was not the church's method to take alleged grievances to the public press, but rather to approach the authorities directly and in a responsible manner.

The commission for liaison with the authorities co-operates regularly and very closely with the commissions for liaison of the daughter churches and is continuing its work in this regard. The Synod assured this commission of its continual prayers to God that He should bless the commission with His guidance in the handling of the problems with which it has to deal.

54. Migrant labour.

54.1 Migrant labour and the economy.

The economic structure of South Africa is to a large extent dependent on the migrant labour system and if this system should suddenly be abolished, it would not only lead to a serious disruption of the economy general and that of the homelands, but would also cause deprivation for the migrant labourers and their families.

A migrant labourer is someone temporarily residing in a city, town or on a farm in order to sell his labour there. He normally enters into a contract with his employer and after the expiry of this contract he returns to his permanent home in one or other of the homelands. This system enables the authorities to control the movement of the large Black labour force in order to avoid an undue concentration of large numbers of labourers and their dependents in one place, which might lead to unemployment and slum conditions. Migrant labour and influx control in the cities are inseparable – facets of one system. If migrant labour were to be abolished while influx control were maintained to prevent chaos in the labour market, there would be total economic collapse and famine in the homelands because these are not as yet capable of providing a livelihood for their populations without the additional income of the migrant labourers.

Abolition of both migrant labour system and influx control will not only promote chaos in the labour market but will also bring all development in the homelands to a virtual halt because the Bantu in the homelands will flock to the cities.

In 1969 some 2,5 million Black labourers were legally employed in White urban areas. Of these, 500 000 were domestic servants. More than half of the 2,5 million labourers were migrant workers. Moreover, the ratio of migrant labourers to those living with their families in the urban areas was rising (F. Wilson: **Migrant Labour in S.A.,** p. 77).

If this system should be continued and even extended to an unlimited extent, the homelands would certainly suffer in the long run. The migrant labour system reinforces the tendency among the Bantu not to make a contribution to the development of their homelands: the homeland remains economically dependent upon other areas and does not gain economic viability in its own right. Moreover, the labourers tend to move about doing mostly unskilled labour on a temporary, contractual basis – which inevitably retards the development of a conservative middle class, so essential for a sound national life.

54.2 Migrant labour disrupts family life.

The migrant labour system is one of the factors which disrupt the stability of marriage and family life among the Bantu.

Migratory labour leads inter alia to the break-up of families, the separation of couples legally married, neglect and disruption of family life, moral deprivation, etc. Since these consequences of the migratory labour system are well-known and have been exhaustively dealt with in various reports of the church, we need not discuss them in detail here. (For factual data on the system and its consequences we would refer the reader to the following: Handelinge van die Nederduise Gereformeerde Kerk in Suid-Afrika, 1965; Handelinge van die Derde Algemene Sinode van die Ned. Geref. Kerk in Afrika, 1971; and F. Wilson: **Migrant Labour in South Africa.**)

54.3 Migrant labour and the establishment of congregations.

The migrant labour system creates problems for the church in its efforts to establish proper and stable congregations. A sound family life is an essential prerequisite for a sound church organisation.

The establishment of stable congregations is virtually impossible either in the homeland or in urban areas. Because their presence in the urban areas is only temporary, it is difficult to provide them with a meaningful religious life. The temporary nature of their sojourn also has a deleterious effect on their attitude: they find it virtually impossible to associate themselves with any local activities of the church. In addition, the congregations in the homelands suffer because there are too few men around: there are not enough fathers to exercise the spiritual and psychological discipline necessary for a sound church life. In fact, there can be no sound church life where there is no sound family life.

54.4 The consequences of the migrant labour system.

Although the migrant labour system cannot be said to be contrary to the teachings of the Bible, as such it should be eliminated as far as possible to avoid its disruptive consequences.

54.5 Development of the homelands.

A radical acceleration in the development and consolidation of the homelands can be a significant factor in finally eliminating the whole migratory labour system. The governing authorities and the economic sectors of the country should be encouraged to undertake such a programme. It is also essential to train more Black technicians and entrepreneurs.

55. The church and the migrant labour system.

55.1 Development of Black leaders.

Both church and state have a major role to play in the education and development of Black leaders to take the initiative in the development of the homelands so that dependency on migrant labour may as far as possible be eliminated.

55.2 The significance of labour.

The church has a comprehensive educational task in order to convince the Black man of the worth and significance of labour as the calling of God to serve His kingdom.

55.3 Meaningful family life.

In this situation it is at all times the task of the church to teach both employers and employees the significance and richness of a Christian marriage and the worth of a meaningful family life and responsible parenthood.

76

55.4 Extension of the labours of the church.

The church will have to extend its work among migrant labourers in the cities and their families in the homelands in order to cast the light of the gospel on all facets of life.

56. The church and social justice for the Coloured community of South Africa.

The requirements in respect of social justice set out in this report are as applicable to any other population group in South Africa as they are to the Coloureds.

Mutatis mutandis, the demands for social justice for Bantu and Asians must also apply in the case of the Coloureds. This general rule is also applicable to the exposition of racial and inter-people relationships in the light of the Bible, as well as matters such as mixed marriages, multiracial services, ecumenical and other relationships between mother, daughter and sister churches, spiritual communion among believers in the White and Coloured population groups, the catholicity and apostolicity of the church and the missionary task of both mother and daughter churches.

For this reason the section dealing specifically with the Coloureds is brief, because the major portion of the report is also applicable to them.

The second reason for the cursory nature of this section of the report is the fact that a goverment commission, the so-called Theron Commission, is at present engaged in a searching and comprehensive study of all matters affecting the Coloured people. At this stage it would be advisable for the church to await the publication of this report. For that reason, as indicated above, only the Biblical and ethical principles described in the commission's report are applied to the Coloured community here.

The Coloureds are in a unique position vis-à-vis Whites, as far as religious and social relationships between the various population groups of South Africa are concerned.

After the Whites, the Coloureds, as a racially mixed community, are the most christianised and westernised population group in the country. They are South Africans by origin and have had a close relationship with the Whites ever since the first settlement at the Cape. Some 92 per cent of the Coloureds are members of Christian churches, and 30 per cent are adherents of the Dutch Reformed Mission Church. About 80 per cent speak Afrikaans. The vast majority share the culture and life-style of the West.

To be sure, there is still a large gap between Whites and Coloureds as far as educational and economic development is concerned. At the same time it should be pointed out that the Coloureds are not one large homogeneous community, but comprise a variety of disparate groups.

Serious problems arising from the position of the Coloureds deserve the consistent attention of the church.

From the beginning of the settlement at the Cape, christianised Coloureds tended to be integrated in White congregations and to participate in White synods. As a result of the missionary effort of various societies, separate, but not exclusive, congregations were established for Coloureds. With only a few exceptions, up to the year 1881, there were no separate congregations for Coloureds in the Dutch Reformed Mission Church. In that year a start was made with the organisation of Coloured congregations into a separate synod. One Coloured congregation is still a member of the Dutch Reformed mother church today.

Up to 1948 the Coloureds of the Cape Province largely shared the same political rights and privileges as Whites. Since that year there has been a radical change in the socio-political position of Coloureds. Although the new dispensation brought certain specific advantages for the Coloured people – such as the clearance of large slum areas, the establishment of their own local authorities, the employment of large numbers in the civil service and the development of substantial housing schemes and educational centres – and although this positive development is continuing, some painful problems have arisen which pose a serious threat to sound interrelationships.

The following problems deserve continued attention, study and action on the part of state and church:

Uncertainty about the Coloureds' political and economic future, which leads to indifference and frustration, and militates against the cultivation of a will to self-development.

The injudicious proclamation of some group areas which cause inconvenience and even privation among the Coloured people.

Although much has been done by the state to pay fair compensation, for instance for church buildings which had to be vacated in White areas, there are many instances in which the compensation was not enough for property which had to be abandoned when certain areas were rezoned for occupation by groups other than Coloureds.

The agitation for the deproclamation of certain group areas already developed by Coloureds gave rise to uncertainty and frustration.

A serious situation has arisen in certain Coloured residential areas as a result of an inevitable delay in the provision of community and recreational facilities after housing schemes have been completed.

The lack of facilities for refreshment and recreation in the metropolitan and urban areas not only causes much inconvenience but also tempts the people to take part in all sorts of questionable activities.

The church notes with appreciation the announcements by the Minister of Bantu Administration and Development that refreshment, recreational and other facilities should be established for non-White labourers in metropolitan and urban areas.

Dissension in the Coloured community hinders and prevents clearly formulated viewpoints, which to a large extent prevents joint action and tends to blunt the initiative for any joint effort at self-development.

The admixture of Bantu with Coloureds creates a very serious problem in many instances. This is dealt with elsewhere in this report.

The wage gap between Coloureds and Whites doing the same work with the same degree of responsibility causes bitterness and a sense of injustice among the former.

The problems caused by the abuse of liquor are among the most serious social evils demanding the continuous attention of the church.

Another problem demanding the serious attention of the church is the need for family planning and the combating of immorality and promiscuity which cause an extremely high illegitimate birth rate.

The uncontrolled influx of large numbers of Coloureds to certain areas (the Orange Free State, for instance) where previously there were only small Coloured communities, creates problems in both housing and labour relations which render the overall problem more acute in certain respects.

Finally, there is the uncertainty among Coloureds as to where they belong as a group. For centuries Coloureds have been traditionally associated with Whites, but recently they started to identify themselves more with Black Power in reaction to a supposed rejection by Whites. Today there is a distinct danger of polarisation of which events at the University of Western Cape in 1973 were symptomatic.

It is clear that this problem is not confined to the university and it seems likely that it will assume more serious proportions in future. **By its very being, calling and influence the church has a unique responsibility in the solution of these problems.**

No other organisation has the advantage of a common bond of faith which is the basis for sound relationships. It is not the function of the church to conjure up a vague or idealistic dream but rather to build firm and tangible bridges, the worth and efficiency of which can stand the test of time. It is imperative that the church become more aware of its strategic position as intermediary between the various population groups, for therein lies an uncompleted deaconal task which may well turn out to be one of the major challenges facing the church in these times.

At the nation-wide missionary congress held in Cape Town in 1972, the discussions in the various study circles were mainly centred on sound relations on a personal level. Most of the motions emphasised the importance of a Christian philosophy of life as basis for relationships between individual members of the various population groups. In this matter there was complete unanimity among both White and Coloured delegates. The need for dialogue and contact between ordinary members of Coloured and White congregations was also emphasised. In all these spheres the church is called upon by the teachings of the Bible to guide, inform and activate its members on the basis of the principles of the Word of God, but it is not called upon or qualified to provide blueprints for the solution of socio-economic or political problems.

57. The church and social justice for Indians and other Asians in South Africa.

The demands for social justice described elsewhere in this report are as much applicable to Indians and other Asians as they are to any other population group in the country.

The Asians of South Africa are a minority group. To them India is as much a foreign country as Britain is to most South African-born English-speaking citizens and the Netherlands, Germany or France is to Afrikaans-speaking citizens We therefore accept that Asians are a permanent part of the multinational community of South Africa. For this reason continuous attention should be given to their religious, social, economic and political needs.

Although a great deal of positive work has been done on behalf of the Asians, there are certain points of friction which create serious problems for this population group and for community relations in general, and in this regard the church is called upon to promote social justice or apply it itself. Some of the problems are the following:

Certain specific problems flowing from the proclamation of group areas, such as a feeling of uncertainty, problems in connection with property and disruption of trade.

Certain limitations on the tenure of land in the case of people who have no "homeland" of their own.

The inadequacy of social services, recreational and other facilities when new residential areas are established for Asians.

80

The effect of job reservation and the wage gap on the development of Asians and on the promotion of sound group relations.

The question of the representation of Asians in general and of Christian Asians in particular on boards of management and other institutions which serve these people.

The problem of the general political future of Asians in South Africa which should continually be reconsidered in order to prevent unrest and a deterioration of group relations.

Restrictions on the movement of Indians and Asians in South Africa.

Chapter 4

Church and Missionary Work

58. The unity of the church and the existence of separate church affiliations for the various population groups.

The existence of separate Dutch Reformed Church affiliations for the various population groups is recognised as being in accordance with the plurality of church affiliations described in the Bible. These enable each individual to hear and preach the great deeds of God in the context of his own language, culture and national affiliation (cf. Algemene Sendingreglement, section 1.3 and 1.4).

That the church comprises separate church affiliations is not in conflict with the essential being of the church as described in the Bible. These multiple church affiliations may, however, not exist in complete isolation from one other, since that would indicate a plurality of the church which would be impermissible because the body of Christ cannot be divided. This plurality is merely designed to serve the church as the body of Christ so that it may thereby develop more fully and more effectively. The plurality is therefore meant to serve the well-being of the church: the plurality is not essential for the being of the church.

The plural system of the Dutch Reformed Church is the result of a pattern which crystallised during a long period in the history of this church. Looking back today, the church cannot but regard the existence of separate Dutch Reformed Church affiliations as a development whereby the interests of the church in South Africa have been well served.

There is an essential unity among the separate Dutch Reformed Church affiliations of the various population groups – in terms of the common belief in and attachment to the same God and His Word, the acceptance of the same Reformed confession and church goverment and also in terms of their historical association (Algemene Sendingreglement, section 18).

According to the New Testament there is only one church of Christ of which He is the Head (Col. 1 : 18), the **summus moderator** (Calvin: **Commentary on Acts** 13 : 2). The unity of the church derives from the common belief in Jesus Christ. In its confession the church gives expression to the fact that Christ is its Head and

Lord and through its church government it seeks to reveal the sovereignty of Christ over the church. Wherever the faithful consider themselves bound to Christ and His Word and accept the same confession in respect of Him, the church is to be found in its unity, and this unity is revealed in particular by the acceptance of the same church government in which the sovereignty of Christ over them finds expression. The establishment of the daughter churches of the Dutch Reformed Church took place under the auspices of the mother church; thus they are historically associated with the mother church.

The essential unity of the separate Dutch Reformed Church affiliations should be professed and maintained through close interrelationships and should at all times be made manifest (Algemene Sendingreglement, section 18).

The unity of the church not only comprises the unity of a mystical association of believers in Christ, but also a concrete, visible fellowship of the faithful with one another. The fellowship of the faithful in Christ with one another is a witness to the world that Christ is of God (John 17).

This fellowship of believers does not, however, mean that it is necessary for believers to be associated in one institutional church structure. After all, there is no reference in the Bible to the need for one church affiliation as a prerequisite for the revelation of the unity of the faithful. The separately constituted Dutch Reformed church affiliations do not necessarily have to be combined into one church affiliation in order to manifest their essential unity in a concrete manner. The unity is not dependent upon one church structure, but upon the fellowship in Christ and the fellowship of the believers in the congregation (local church).

The visible unity of the Dutch Reformed church affiliations should, however, find expression on both the local level and on that of major church gatherings. This means that there should be contact between the members of the various church associations on the personal level and that there should from time to time be meetings of these members for special occasions, as well as mutual consultations in official church meetings.

Separate church affiliations for the various population groups is the policy of the Dutch Reformed Church, but this is not designed to isolate the believers in seperate church affiliations. It originated as missionary policy: in this way the church could effectively penetrate the very existence of the various population groups. It did not, however, imply the denial of the need for mutual contact between members or consultations among the various church affiliations with a view to spiritual growth and powerful testimony. In fact, the Dutch Reformed Church has at all times let it be known that it is its desire that the unity of the church affiliations should be maintained and find expression in close mutual relationships.

For the sake of the full development of the various church affiliations in the common faith, and so that they may bear common testimony in as multinational country, it is necessary that the separate Dutch Reformed church affiliations be officially linked together in federal meetings with a predetermined and clearly defined objective. Where this is not practically possible, contact should be maintained by means of correspondence. This also means that there may be liaison at the consistory, presbytery and synod levels.

The separate Dutch Reformed Church affiliations are the embodiment of only one Dutch Reformed Church which has affiliations among the various population groups. If these affiliations were to exist separately without any official liaison among them, it would mean a contradiction of the existence of the Dutch Reformed Church as one whole.

59. The holiness of the church and the spiritual communion between mother and daughter churches.

Because the church is holy, it belongs to God and exists as a unique institution which should be distinguished from all other institutions in the world, for it is essentially different and autogenous.

The holiness of the church does not entail moral or ethical perfection on the part of those who are members of the church. They are merely the people in whom the provisional and still incomplete manifestation of the new humanity, created and still to be recreated in the image of God, is beginning to take shape. The holiness of the church may, however, not be regarded as an objective quality which the church only possesses before God. Its holiness is an imperative to its members to give subjective expression to the fact that they adopted a new way of life after they had been released from the bondage of sin and death. The church must be a revelation to the world of the victory over the power of sin, the laying down of minority status and the gradual progress towards maturity of the new man. In this the church must show no pretension in respect of its own achievements or worth; it must merely pursue sanctification as the will of God for men. There will naturally be constant tension between the imputed sanctification of the church and the empirical manifestation thereof, but the church is at all times called upon to reveal the concrete existence of its holiness. The revelation of this holiness must assist the church to stand up as prophetic example for the new humanity in the midst of the humanity of the day. Thus the church must always be different from humanity in its sinful existence and this difference must also be manifest in the interrelationship of believers.

The holiness of the church is inter alia also revealed in and nourished by the fellowship of believers.

It is the calling of the church to give manifest expression to the unanimity and love of the believers. Throughout the Bible, and more particularly the New Testament, the believers are called upon to manifest that they are of Christ through their concord, unanimity and brotherly love. It is therefore the sacred calling of the church to make believers aware of their responsibility to bear testimony, through their mutual relationships and fellowship, of the truth and power of the message of Christ. The freedom of believers to practise their fellowship, wherever and whenever it is needed, may therefore never be curtailed or abolished. Whenever the practice of fellowship between members of the mother and daughter churches is curtailed because of tendencies towards an unchristian exclusivism or a malevolent disposition, the believers must consider it their duty to eliminate these circumstances.

Spiritual communion or fellowship is experienced inter alia where the believers are gathered in fellowship with Christ through His Word and Spirit. This fellowship may also be practised on occasion where believers from various churches are gathered to worship together. How this should be effected in practice, is the responsibility of the local church council.

Spiritual communion is primarily the communion between God and the believing worshipper through the Word and Spirit of God. The spiritual fellowship of believers is based on and flows from this.

But the manner in which God speaks to his children through his Word and Spirit will to a certain degree depend upon the national identity of the person or people concerned. Language and culture play a significant role in this communion. By the very nature of things, each ethnic group must practise its religion within the context of its own language and culture.

How these particular occasions should be organised, is the responsibility of the local church council which must approach the matter with wisdom to ensure that the purpose of the gathering is not defeated by the manner of the gathering.

As soon as specific guide lines are laid down, the practice of spiritual fellowship is formalised and become forced. Spiritual fellowship should never be formalised or regimented. There is always only one ruling principle: the reality of faith in Christ through his Word and

Spirit, based on a common confession. Ecumenical idealism which would seek to achieve more than this, runs the risk of limiting the fellowship in Christ which already exists through his Word and Spirit, or of formalising human relationships in accordance with a specific conviction. Specific political convictions are responsible for much of the confused thinking at the ecumenical level of theology today. And this has promoted neither ecumenical interests nor sound relations because such actions militate against the spontaneity of spiritual fellowship.

60. The catholicity of the church and the indigenous distinctiveness of the church among the various peoples.
The Church of Christ is universal.
The Greek word for universal or catholic is **kata-holos** which literally means according to the whole, comprising the whole or concerned with the whole. The word itself does not appear in the Bible, but the concept does. The following aspects of catholicity, in particular, are emphasized:
With regard to the world: The church should embrace the entire populated earth; it should not be limited to one country or one particular people. Thus, the church should not become so bound up in one particular cultural milieu that it would bear a foreign character in other cultures. The missionary mandate embraces the entire earth until the fullness of time.
With regard to truth: We are concerned here with the all embracing nature of the truth which has been entrusted to the church through revelation. This does not, however, safeguard the church against error, nor does it relieve it of the duty to exercise continuous exegesis. Nevertheless, it is a guarantee against **relativism** (which teaches that absolute truth is nowhere to be found), and against **syncretism,** which teaches all religions together contain the truth and each individual religion only part thereof. Where the Spirit of God does not lead in truth and where the foundation of the prophets and the apostles is absent, there can be no question of a catholic gathering of believers.
With regard to obedience: The universality of the church is also found in its own bosom. No limit is set to its obedience and dedication. The church must love God with all its heart, soul and mind and it must love its neighbour as itself. A catholic faith is one that manifests itself in every sphere and situation of life and in answer to every problem of life.
The Christian faith is universal: it is our duty to localise its universality.
In Chapter 1 of this report on human relations in a Scriptural

perspective we stated, 'The New Testament refers to the diversity of peoples without any negative disqualification' and added the following explanation, 'Without revoking or questioning the equality or solidarity of the various peoples, the New Testament accepts the fact of the existence of disparate peoples (Matthew 28 : 19; Acts 2 : 5 et seq.; Romans 1 : 16, etc.)'. 'The natural diversity of man and people survives in the Church of Christ but is sanctified in Him', with, inter alia, the following motivation: 'The missionary commission (Matthew 28 : 19) states that the gospel should be brought to the nations, in keeping with the promise to Abraham (Gen. 12 : 3, 22 : 18)'." By this we mean that the various peoples are not denationalised to a homogeneity which denies cultural identities, linguistic barriers and the psychological distinctiveness of each people. Further confirmation of this is found in Paul's approach to missionary work: he came as a Jew among Jews to win them over. Moreover, the great language miracle of Whit Sunday confirms that it is the will of God that each man should learn of the great deeds of God in his own language. In Europe and the Americas Christianity has been "westernised" and in the Orthodox Churches it has been orientalised; by the same token the Christian faith must be Africanised in Africa. When the church becomes truly indigenous, it does not imply syncretism or an adulteration of Biblical truths. On the contrary, it gives expression to the catholicity of Christendom because it speaks to all peoples in all languages.

Evangelisation is an act through which the universality of the Christian faith is proclaimed. Making the church indigenous means localising the gospel within a specific environment.

It is of vital importance to the young churches that their becoming indigenous should be **Christo-centric.** Their true being as churches is in Christ and not in their being indigenous. Localising the faith means "translating" the universal applicability of the Christian faith into the language best understood by the people of a given area. "Parthians and Medes and Elamites ... were all amazed and marvelled, saying to one another; Behold, are not all these which speak Galileans? And how hear we every man in our own tongue, wherein we were born?" (Acts 2 : 5-13). That was the beginning of localisation, which goes hand in hand with spreading the gospel. Africa cannot be evangelised in western languages or through the Christendom of the East. "This has been done far too long, and few Africans can claim that they hear each in his own language the mighty works of God. There lies the great challenge for the church in our continent" (J. S. Mbiti: **Christianity and Traditional Religions in Africa** IRM, October 1970, p. 431).

87

The Study Report: Race Relations, submitted to the Reformed Ecumenical Synod in 1968, contains the following passage: "In the mission work of the church there should be no imposition of the elements of one culture upon another, although there can be no objection to the voluntary adoption of such elements. There should, on the other hand, be no acquiescence by Christians in a culture which has been thoroughly shaped by a non-Christian religion. The requirements of the Word should be paramount. The evangelical principle should work as a yeast in each culture to give it such form that the ethos thereby formed is worthy of the Gospel (Phil. 1 : 27).

"The requirement that the younger church should develop in accordance with the background, character and culture of its own people does not result from any particular political ideology, but from that Christian love for the neighbour which accepts his person for the sake of Christ. The same principle requires the training of the younger church to self-government under the headship of Christ and the full acceptance of its members as equals for Christ's sake.

"In obedience to the mission mandate of Christ, the church must bring the gospel to all nations regardless of race. The principle of love for the neighbour requires that this mission respect the character and culture of the recipients of the gospel so that new churches may come to self-expression in harmony with Scripture."

Condemnation or neglect of, or contempt for, a particular culture would amount to a division between nature and grace, according to which the world of the Black man would be the unhallowed heathen area where Satan reigns supreme with his unholy spirits while God has given his holy church to one particular culture and has cast his message into one particular language which whould be the mould for every other community which accepted the church. The Reformation revolted against the Roman concept some four and a half centuries ago and declared that the revelation which appeared in Christ was definitely not in conflict with nature but merely opposed to sin which has penetrated creation as a foreign element (Cf. Bavinck: **Gereformeerde Dogmatiek** 1, p. 330-331).

As far as Africa is concerned, the church has a major task among the indigenous peoples: to express an opinion on the eventual christianisation of community relationships and cultural customs such as lobola, the status of women, initiation and other similar customs. Customs which cannot be reconciled with the gospel, such as polygamy, ancestor worship, witchcraft, etc., must be condemned. It is, however, a matter of principle that the younger churches should not be made indigenous by the old church: they should become indigenous on their own initiative and their own Christian vitality, and should take possession of certain specific community customs.

The design of the indigenous church and the application of the principle of being indigenous are not in the first place the functions of the missionary. He is, however, the important and essential organ who initiates, encourages and inspires through true and faithful preaching in the language of the people among whom he works.

Soltau states: "Too often the idea of establishing or building a church has been emphasised with the thought uppermost that the missionary, like the builder, must lay in place each stone until the work is nearly complete. In reality, the missionary has the responsibility for only the part of the seed-sowing and then cultivation of the young plants, but the church itself grows by the power of the Holy Spirit" (T. S. Soltau, **Missions at the Crossroads: the indigenous church – a solution for the unfinished task,** 1963, p. 11).

There are three aspects to the way in which a church becomes indigenous:

The abandoment of customs and practices which cannot be reconciled with the essence of the gospel. A thorough study of the Bible and obedient submission to God's word is necessary to achieve this.

The purification and cleansing of customs and practices which are not basic to the ethnic religion but give expression to the identity of the people who are claimed by the gospel to the glory of God and therefore must be christianised.

The creation of new distinctive cultural practises which fit the national identity and in which the African can express himself. A careful study should be made of the manner in which separatism has created a religious sounding-board for the people of Africa. An answer should be provided to the question whether the established churches took sufficient account of certain ontological and cosmological elements which are respected by the various separatist movements. In this connection we are, in particular, thinking of the need of the Black man for liaison, the meaning of marriage, sex, birth, the need for vitality, etc.

61. The apostolicity of the church and the missionary task of mother and daughter churches.

The church of Christ is a missionary church.

The triune God uses the church for the gathering of His chosen people and the coming of His kingdom (cf. Algemene Sendingreglement, section 1.1). Christ was sent to the world by the Father and the church exists in Him as a missionary church. The Holy Ghost which bears testimony for Christ and glorifies Him, animates, confirms and compels the church at all times to bear testimony as a missionary church. The mission mandate compels the church to be a missionary church, which it is in Christ. The living church is always a missionary church.

The church is a missionary church wherever and in whatever group of people it may exist.

No church can exist in Christ unless it is filled with missionary zeal. Wherever on earth and in whatever group of people the church may exist, it can be a true church only if it bears testimony and acts as missionary church. This applies in all circumstances and at all times, for both mother and daughter churches.

The church has a missionary function in the world.

The church has a missionary function within its own ranks as well as in the world beyond its own borders. This applies to both mother and daughter churches. Certain mother and daughter churches may find themselves in the position where their missionary function is performed chiefly within their own ranks. This would be the case where a church is situated within its own missionary field. If a daughter church does not have large missionary funds at its disposal, the obvious course to follow would be a spontaneous missionary action among its own members.

A church may undertake its missionary action either independently or as a joint effort of mother and daughter churches.

Missionary activities are often more efficient when they are undertaken jointly rather than separately (cf. the motto of the meeting of the International Missionary Council at Whiteby in 1947: **"Partners in obedience"**). It is often desirable that mother and daughter churches which are closely related to one another in confession and history, undertake their missionary action on a joint basis. This also applies to the Dutch Reformed mother and daughter churches.

A joint missionary action by mother and daughter church may be undertaken either locally or as a joint effort elsewhere.

When missionary action is undertaken jointly by mother and daughter churches, it should be governed by a mutual agreement. At times it may be desirable that the joint missionary action be controlled by a liaison commission on which both mother and daughter churches are represented. It may also be desirable for such a joint effort to be under the control chiefly of the council of the daughter church, while the mother church continues to render financial assistance and provide the necessary manpower.

90

Should there be an overlapping in mission congregations between mother and daughter church, it is essential that the local missionary effort be undertaken jointly and after joint consultations.

In the event of a joint local missionary action by mother and daughter churches, care should be taken that the missionary action of one is not obstructed by that of the other.
Local missionary actions are undertaken within the province of both mother and daughter congregations where each thus has its own missionary obligations. It is imperative that there should be joint consultations and planning in these cases. The interests of the kingdom of God and of the many people without Christ should, however, be of paramount importance at all times. It may, for instance, happen that the daughter church is small and has little experience in the missionary field. In such a case it would be in the interests of God's kingdom to give the mother congregation the full and unfettered opportunity of reaching the unchristianised groups with the gospel of Christ.

Agreements for joint missionary actions should be determined by the church councils concerned, according to the demands of the prevailing circumstances.
The General Synod may lay down certain guide-lines for such agreements, but the church managements, councils, presbyteries or Synods of the mother and daughter churches must work out the details of these agreements.

The mother and daughter churches should deliberate jointly on the status and service of the missionary within the daughter church.
There is a divergence of opinion on this matter in both mother and daughter churches. Therefore it is essential that mother and daughter churches should deliberate further on this, both independently and jointly. The Federal Council of the Dutch Reformed Church could serve as an instrument for such joint deliberations at which all missionary and church situations should be taken into account, as well as the need for the expansion of the kingdom of God and the spiritual well-being of the daughter church.

Whenever a joint missionary action is planned by mother and daughter churches in an area where well-disposed kindred churches are also engaged in missionary work, there should be joint deliberations to avoid overlapping in the missionary effort.
Churches which are spiritually closely related to one another in confession and historical background should give expression to their

unity in Christ through mutual recognition in their missionary actions. Interference in one another's missionary fields without joint deliberations and mutual agreements is not permissible. This destroys the experience of unity and weakens the impact of the missionary effort. These churches should rather consider how they could support one another's missionary efforts.

Chapter 5

Marriage and Mixed Marriage

62. The concept "marriage".

Holy Scripture defines marriage as a most intimate love relationship between one man and one woman who should be suited to one another in every respect. If two people are not thus suited to one another, marriage between them would be in conflict with Biblical precepts for a true marriage.

Before we can decide what a "mixed" marriage is, we should first determine what marriage is. Holy Scripture defines marriage as a most intimate love relationship between one man and one woman who should be suited to one another in every respect. If two people are not thus suited to one another, marriage between them would be in conflict with Biblical precepts for a true marriage (Gen. 2 : 18; Matthew 19 : 4-6).

63. The concept "mixed marriages".

The concept "mixed marriages" is derived from matrimonial ethics and in this report it refers to marriages between persons of different racial or ethnic groups. In the Bible the concept relates to the problem of miscegenation between Israel and the heathen nations by which it was surrounded and, in this sense, it was fundamentally a religious problem. A study of Biblical data reveals that while, on the one hand, the Israelites were forbidden to marry the heathens in their vicinity, there was, on the other hand, nevertheless miscegenation on a comparatively large scale, although it was not normative in all cases.

The concept is derived from matrimonial ethics where it is used in reference to marriages between persons of different confessions or church affiliations (Roman Catholics and Protestants), between Christians and Jews and, more particularly, between Christians and heathens. In this study the term is used in reference to marriages between persons of different racial and ethnic groups.

The term presupposes that in such marriages irreconcilable elements in respect of religion, race and culture are joined together.

63.1 Biblical data:

The Biblical data to be considered here are concerned with the problem of miscenegation between Israel and the heathen nations in its midst and vicinity. In the light of Israel's unique position and calling as bearer of the promise of salvation in a heathen environment, the problem in this case is fundamentally religious. Since th ethnic aspect of Israel's existence also impinges on the problem, one would expect the Bible to be explicit also in this respect.

A study of Biblical data reveals that the people of God were forbidden to marry heathens from their vicinity (Gen. 24 : 3; 28 : 1; 6 : 8; Ex. 23; 23-33; 34 : 10-17; Num. 33 : 50-56; Deut. 7 : 1; 20 : 16; 25 : 17-19; Esra 9 : 3, 5-15, 10-1; Neh. 13 : 25, 28). At the same time miscegenation occurred on a large scale (Gen. 21, 25, 29, 30; 38 : 2; 41 : 45, 50; 46 : 10, 20; 48 : 5; Ex. 2 : 21; Num. 12 : 1; 1 Kings 11 : 1-3, etc.; cf. the article "matrimoniom Mixtum" in NGTT, June 1961, p. 153-169, for a discussion of Biblical data which have to be considered in this respect).

63.2 Religious motivation:

The key to a proper perspective on and interpretation of Biblical data lies in the religious motive. The prohibition of "mixed marriages" in Scripture is in the first place concerned with the preservation of the mystery of Israel's existence and destiny as chosen people of the Lord. Thus in Gen. 24 : 3, 4 and in Gen. 28 : 1, 6, 8 Isaac and Jacob are respectively forbidden to marry the daughters of the Canaanites. This was the motive for the extermination of the Canaanites and the prohibition of marriages with them: "lest they make thee sin against me: for if thou serve their gods, it will surely be a snare unto thee" (Ex. 23 : 33). ". . . and their daughters go a whoring after their gods, and make thy sons go a whoring after their gods" (Ex. 34 : 16). "For they will turn away thy sons from following me, that they may serve other gods.| . ." (Deut. 7 : 4). Solomon's marriage with strange women (1 Kings 11 : 1-13) caused him to sin (Neh. 13 : 26).

There can be no difference in interpretation on this point. Where the Bible specifically proscribes "mixed marriages", it does so in the first place on religious grounds.

63.3 "Racial" considerations.

Consensus: Various study commissions of the Dutch Reformed Church, as well as the Reformed Ecumenical Synod (RES) of Lunteren, 1968, (p. 124, 126), came to the conclusion that the Bible does not, in so many words, pronounce upon racially mixed marriages. The **Acts and Reports** of the afore-mentioned synod contain the following statement: ". . . Scripture neither directly prescribes nor prohibits racially mixed marriages" (p. 124), etc. "Holy Scripture makes no pronouncement on racially mixed marriages" (p. 126). These pronouncements are indeed in accordance with the facts. "There is no direct pronouncement in Scripture which either approves or condemns racially mixed marriages" **(Report of the Ad Hoc Commission on Mixed Marriages).**

Problematical aspects:

In considering the ethnic and racial aspects of the problem, one should bear in mind that, in the first place, the Bible is not meant to serve as a manual for anthropology, sociology or eugenics; that, secondly, it is not always easy to determine the degree of kinship or racial differences between the two partners of a "mixed marriage"; and that, thirdly, the general unitary culture of modern times has considerably eased the contracting of "mixed marriages".

Degree of racial difference:

In general we may state that most "mixed marriages" mentioned in the Bible were contracted between persons racially related to one another (i.a. Num. 31; Judges 3 : 6; 1 Chron. 5 : 21, etc.). In a few instances, the marriages are obviously between persons of different racial origin, as in the case of Moses and the Ethiopian woman he had married (Numbers 12 : 1). It is true that the Simite-Hamitic peoples are considered to belong to the same family, at least linguistically. In the paragraph on the "racial situation" in Israel we pointed out that elements of all sorts of races were present in the Holy Land. Fact of the matter is, there is no pronouncement in Holy Scripture which either prohibits or encourages purely on racial grounds marriages with persons from these racial groups.

63.4 Norm and practice

We would also draw attention to the fact that in considering the "mixed marriages" in Israel, we should distinguish between norm and practice. We may assume that most of these marriages probably occurred in conflict with the letter and/or the spirit of the prohibition. In determining a norm for considering such marriages, one should take cognisance of the unique position of isolation of Israel as the chosen people of God (Ex. 19 : 5) and the primarily spiritual nature of its existence and its destiny as bearer of the Lord's promise of salvation. Therefore, the specific prohibition of mixed marriages has, in the case of Israel, primarily a religious basis.

The word of Paul was as much applicable to the members of the chosen people as to the church of the New Testament: "Be ye not unequally yoked together with unbelievers" (2 Cor. 6 : 14, 15). For Israel this was either the explicit or implied norm according to which the practice had to be judged. The fact that Israel was at the same time a nation among nations could possibly have been an implied part of that norm, but, for various reasons, we may not overemphasise the significance thereof. In the first place, Israel's isolation in the Bible is not dependent upon its autogenous national or racial identity but upon God's merciful choice of and his covenant with this people (Ex. 19 : 5, 6; 24 : 3-8; Deut. 7 : 6-8, etc.). Secondly, it is evident that when members of other nations, such as Ruth and Jarha (1 Cron. 2 : 34-36), identified themselves with the chosen people, i.e. in its **character as the people of God,** and therefore with the religion of Israel, the prohibition of mixed marriages obviously did not apply. This supposition is strengthened when, in the third place, we consider the fact that the law allowed miscegenation in both directions: through circumcision it was in principle possible for foreigners to be absorbed into Israel's community of peoples (Ex. 12 : 8; Numbers 9 : 14; 15 : 14-16); and in the many wars women and children were carried away as prisoners of war and the law decreed that the unmarried ones could be considered booty. In Deut. 21 : 10-14 marriages with such women are presupposed, since the precept of these verses serves to protect the position of such women. That Israel did, in fact, carry off young girls from other peoples, even on a massive scale (32 000!), is revealed in e.a. Numbers 31 : 9 et seq. Whatever conclusion we may come to in respect of the data on mixed marriages in the Old Testament, the fact remains that national identity and racial considerations obviously did not play a decisive role in the determination of the norm. This does not, however, mean that national identity and racial considerations were of no importance in this connection. After all, we accept that ethnic diversity is the will of God and that the mandate to cultivate the earth also applies to the various peoples. Fact of the matter, however, is that we may not rely on the position of isolation of Israel for the determination of a norm in this respect, for that position has an essentially religious basis.

64. Points of agreement and difference.

In all considerations of racial and inter-people relations, high priority is given to the problem of the racially mixed marriage. In this paragraph we shall concentrate on points of both difference and agreement in order to come to a better understanding of this problem.

64.1 Points of agreement.

There seems to be agreement on at least two points within the ranks of churches belonging to the RES: the fact that the Biblical prohibition of "racially mixed" marriages has a predominantly religious motivation and that the Bible does not literally pronounce either in favour of or against such marriages.

Within the ranks of churches belonging to the RES there seems to be agreement on at least two points. The first is that the prohibition in Israel on "racially mixed" marriages has a predominantly religious motivation. The second is that the Bible does not pronounce in so many words either for or against such racially mixed marriages, except for this religious motivation.

64.2 Points of difference.

There is, however, a difference of opinion on the role of church and state in the contracting of such marriages. According to the RES of Lunteren, church and state should not prohibit such marriages for they have no right to limit the free choice of a marriage partner. This conclusion is patently one-sided as well as an oversimplification of the facts. A marriage is in the first instance a personal and family affair, but it also has social, religious and politico-juridical significance; therefore such a marriage does not fall entirely outside the concern of society, church and state. In the first two instances the "interference" would not be of a decisive nature – in the sense that society and the church would prohibit such racially mixed marriages. This does not mean, however, that society and the church have no interest in the contracting of such a marriage. As far as the church is concerned, it most certainly has a pastoral calling to warn against the contracting of such marriages in certain circumstances and in a particular social structure to which racially mixed marriages are foreign. This warning would be essentially pastorally motivated, in view of the unfavourable complications of such a marriage for the partners themselves, but more particularly for their progeny.

The position of the authorities in this regard is quite different. In normal circumstances it is certainly not the function of the authorities to interfere in the free choice of marriage partners. And yet it is quite possible and conceivable that the authorities would in certain circumstances prohibit the contracting of such marriages. In the stabilisation of relationships in a multiracial and multinational situation, the equilibrium may be disturbed by the contracting of racially mixed marriages and in these circumstances the preservation of "peace" in the Biblical sense would be of more importance to the authorities than the free choice of marriage partners by certain in-

dividuals. But this should at all times be seen as an extraordinary measure and this prohibition should, as a matter of course, be reviewed whenever circumstances permit it.

The points of difference concern the role of church and state in the contracting of racially mixed marriages. The relevant resolution of the RES (Lunteren) reads as follows, "Holy Scripture does not give a judgment about racially mixed marriages; contracting a marriage is primarily a personal and family concern. Church and state should refrain from prohibiting racially mixed marriages, because they have no right to limit the free choice of a marriage partner" (No. 12, p. 65, 340).

We do not agree with the conclusion in the second part of the resolution: it is one-sided as well as an oversimplification of the facts. We do concede that marriage is primarily a personal and family affair, but at the same time the Bible teaches that a marriage is not merely the private concern of two people or of their families. The parents have a say, not only within the line of the covenant (Abraham, Isaac and Jacob) but also outside the line of the covenant (Esau, Gen. 26 : 34-35; 28 : 8). The family and the national group and therefore also its government, as well as the mouthpiece in the religious field – these are all concerned with the marriage between any given couple. The church most certainly has a pastoral calling to warn against the dangers and complications of such a marriage in certain circumstances and to do everything in its power to discourage it.

We do agree, however, that in normal circumstances it is not the function of the state (government) to interfere in the freedom of choice of a marriage partner. Yet it is quite possible and conceivable that in certain circumstances the government may prohibit the contracting of such marriages. It is the function of the government to preserve order in society and when it decides for certain reasons that in a multiracial and multinational society public order is best preserved by the separate existence of the various population groups, or when the government is convinced that public order is threatened by the contracting of mixed marriages, the prohibition of mixed marriages may be justified as an aspect of this policy. But the fact remains that this would be an extraordinary measure and it goes without saying that the prohibition would be reviewed when circumstances permitted such a step.

65. Basic considerations.

In considering racially mixed marriages one should take cognisance of the following:

98

Such marriages are physically possible.

Factors which impede the happiness and full development of a Christian marriage and those which would eventually destroy the God-given diversity and identity, would render such a marriage undesirable and impermissible. Such factors are manifest when there are substantial differences between the two partners in respect of religion, social structure, cultural pattern, biological descent, etc.

Such marriages are undesirable for as long as the impeding factors exist.

In considering racially mixed marriages, account should also be taken of the following considerations:

The fact that such marriages are physically possible, in terms of the unity of the human race which embraces, inter alia, the physical similarity of all races and the fact that they can interbreed.

The fact that, according to the Bible, marriage is a most intimate relationship between a man and a woman willed by God (Gen. 2 : 18, 24). It comprises man entire in his physical, spiritual and social existence and conjoins the partners into a two-in-one way.

From this it follows that any factor which might impede the unification would prevent the marriage from becoming a union in the meaning of the Bible. This means that differences and contrasts, such as might exist between two people from the same population group, and to a greater degree between two people from different population and racial groups, will be an obstacle and will endanger the consummation of the union or even **destroy it completely in proportion as the differences and contrasts become greater.**

Among the factors which render a racially mixed marriage undesirable, there are the historical, ethnic, cultural, and biological factors which contribute towards the creation of a specific social structure and cultural situation.

The command to inhabit and cultivate the earth is not given to the individual only, but also to peoples and nations (cf. Revelation, 21 : 24, 26) and this means that nations should jealously guard the spiritual and cultural treasures which they have acquired in the course of centuries and which, in the case of the Republic of South Africa **endow the White and non-White peoples with their specific and various identities.**

In the Republic of South Africa these factors are naturally of decisive significance.

Should the factors which impede a proper marriage relationship, however, be removed by a process of acculturation, a marriage can, in view of what Scripture says, be regarded as permissible.